Dictionary of
Legal Terms

BROCKHAMPTON PRESS
LONDON

This edition published 1997 by Brockhampton Press, a member of Hodder Headline PLC Group.

ISBN 1 86019 710 8

Printed and bound in the UK.

abandonment (1) the giving up of a legal right, especially the ownership of property, with the intention of not reclaiming it. (2) the relinquishing of all or part of a claim being made under civil law. (3) the leaving by its parent or guardian of a child without proper provision for its care.

abatement the interruption of civil proceedings because of a change of interest or status of one of the parties to the action. If the cause of the action continues, new proceedings may be brought.

abdication the relinquishing of a position held, as that of King Edward VIII in 1936 for which there was no PRECEDENT.

abduction (1) wrongfully taking away a person by force. (2) taking away a girl below the age of 16. (3) in Scots law, taking away an unmarried girl of less than 18 for unlawful sexual purposes.

abet *see* AID OR ABET.

abjuration renunciation by means of an OATH.

abode, right of the right to live in the United Kingdom and to come and go without hindrance.

abortion the termination of a pregnancy before completion, an offence unless the provisions of the Abortion Act 1967 and the Abortion Regulations 1991 are complied with.

abscond to fail to surrender to the custody of a court in order to avoid legal proceedings.

absolute discharge allowing a person convicted of an offence to escape punishment. *See also* DISCHARGE.

absolute insolvency *see* INSOLVENCY.

absolute privilege a defence against a charge of DEFAMATION on the grounds that the statement was made in Parliament, in judicial proceedings or in the fair and accurate reporting, by the media, of judicial proceedings.

absolute title the ownership of land accompanied by a guarantee by the state that no other party has a superior claim to that land.

absolve to release from an obligation.

abuse of process the use of legal process other than for its proper use, e.g. to annoy another party.

ACAS *see* ADVISORY, CONCILIATION AND ARBITRATION SERVICE.

acceleration clause in a loan agreement, a provision that if instalments to repay the debt are not paid by the agreed dates, the whole outstanding debt becomes repayable at once.

acceptance agreement to the terms of an offer, which must be given before the offer has lapsed, must be on the same terms as the offer, must be unconditional and must be given to the party making the offer; in relation to goods, that the buyer has exercised his right to examine them to ascertain that they conform to the terms agreed with the vendor.

acceptance of service a written statement by a SOLICITOR accepting service and undertaking to appear for a CLIENT.

access the freedom to have contact with a child where, after separation or divorce, custody has been awarded to the child's other parent.

accession (1) succeeding to the throne. (2) holding a person responsible for a crime even when that person is not the principal perpetrator of the offence (*see* ACCESSORY). (3) in Scots law, ownership of something attached to something else already owned, e.g. part of a building.

accessory a person who is held responsible for a crime even though not the principal perpetrator of the offence. An *accessory before the fact* is a person who orders or assists the crime; an *accessory after the fact* is a person who harbours or assists in the escape of the principal perpetrator. A person present during the committing of a crime but not taking part in it may be referred to as a *principal in the second degree.*

accomplice a person who takes part in the committing of a criminal offence or who acts as an ACCESSORY.

accord and satisfaction an agreement that discharges an obligation by the offer of a consideration that is not part of the obligation from which release is sought.

accounts a statement of the audited financial position of a LIMITED COMPANY, which is required to be circulated annually to members and which must give a fair and accurate picture of the balance sheet and profit and loss account under the terms of the Companies Acts.

accretion the addition of new land to the boundaries of a state by natural or human means. In Scots law, the term used to describe the natural process is *alluvio.*

accusatorial procedure a procedure in the resolving of disputes in which one party challenges the other in court. The JUDGE acts as a form of umpire to ensure fair play and that proper procedure is followed and points of law observed. *See also* INQUISITORIAL PROCEDURE.

accused a person charged with the committing of a crime.

acquiescence explicit or implicit consent to an action that might otherwise have given grounds for action.

acquisitive prescription *see* PRESCRIPTION.

acquittal the decision by a court that a person prosecuted for a criminal offence is not guilty of that offence. In Scots law, acquittal includes the verdict of NOT PROVEN.

action (1) proceedings by which a legal right is pursued in a CIVIL COURT. (2) civil proceedings in the HIGH COURT initiated by WRIT.

active trust a TRUST that requires a TRUSTEE to perform certain duties.

act of God an event or accident attributable to natural causes (such as flood, earthquake, etc), which no person could reasonably have been expected to anticipate.

Act of Parliament a bill that has passed through all its stages (first and second readings, committee stage, report stage and third reading) and has received the ROYAL ASSENT, whereupon it becomes law.

act of state an act done to another state or to a person not owing allegiance to the state, such as the waging of war.

actual bodily harm the impairment of the health or comfort of a person through the inflicting of hurt or injury, which need not be serious or permanent but is not trifling.

actual notice *see* NOTICE.

adduce to bring forward or present, e.g. evidence to support a statement already made.

ademption the cancellation or reduction of a specific legacy when the sum or item specified is no longer part of the testator's estate or a proportion of it has already been given to the legatee.

adjective law or **adjectival law** the part of the law that relates to court procedure and practice. *See also* SUBSTANTIVE LAW.

adjournment the postponing of the hearing of a case, either to a specified future date, or, if *sine die*, indefinitely.

adjudication (1) the formal judgment of a court or tribunal. (2) in Scots law, a process that can be used to take away heritable property from debtors.

administration order (1) court action designed to maintain an insolvent company as a going concern under the terms of the Insolvency Act 1986, and to appoint an ADMINISTRATOR to manage the business for as long as the order is in force. (2) a court order made for the administration of the assets of a debtor, during which creditors may only claim through the court.

administrative receiver a receiver or manager of a company's property, appointed by or on behalf of the holders of DEBENTURES in the company.

administrator (1) a person appointed to manage a business in financial difficulties through the application of an administrator order. (2) a person appointed by a court to collect and distribute the estate of a deceased person who has died intestate (*see* INTESTACY), or who has not appointed EXECUTORS, or whose executors are unwilling to act.

admissibility the determination that evidence may be offered to a court because it has passed the test of relevance to the action.

adoption a legal process by which the rights and responsibilities of a child's natural parents are transferred to other parties, who become the adoptive parents. An adopted child cannot be designated illegitimate. An adopted child becomes a British citizen if either or both adoptive parents are British citizens.

adoption order a court order conferring parental responsibilities on parties adopting a child.

adult a person aged 18 or over. *See also* MAJORITY.

adultery sexual intercourse between a married partner and another party of the opposite sex, who is not the spouse. In a DIVORCE petition, adultery can constitute the ground 'irretrievable breakdown'.

ad valorem in proportion to the value of something. An *ad valorem* tax is calculated as a proportion of the subject of the tax.

adversarial procedure the court system under which parties to a dispute, or their representatives, are responsible for gathering and presenting EVIDENCE.

adverse possession the occupation by a person of land, which infringes the rightful claims of the true owner.

adverse witness a witness who gives evidence unfavourable to the party who called him but whose credibility may not be questioned. *See also* HOSTILE WITNESS.

Advisory, Conciliation and Arbitration Service (ACAS) a body created by Parliament to help in the resolution of industrial disputes. It also participates in INDUSTRIAL TRIBUNALS.

advocate (1) a person who argues a case in court on behalf of a client. (2) in Scotland, the equivalent of a BARRISTER, with exclusive rights to represent clients in the higher courts. Lay men and women may appear as advocates in tribunals.

Advocate General in European courts, a member of the COURT OF JUSTICE, who assists the court by presenting opinions and arguments that are in the interest of the European Union.

affidavit a written statement that may be presented as evidence. It must be sworn in the presence of a COMMISSIONER FOR OATHS, or a NOTARY PUBLIC in Scotland.

affinity the relationship between a husband or wife and the blood relatives of his or her spouse. *See also* CONSANGUINITY.

affirm (1) to confirm a judgment made by a lower court. (2) to make a declaration that does not invoke the name of God, in place of an OATH.

affirmative pregnant an assertion in PLEADINGS implying or not denying a negative. *See* NEGATIVE PREGNANT.

affray using or threatening to use unlawful violence, other than simply verbal, which would cause a person to fear for his or her safety. The offence may be committed in public or private; it is not necessary for the person threatened to be present.

aforethought planned or deliberate, not spontaneous. *See* MALICE AFORETHOUGHT.

agency a legal arrangement under the terms of which one person acts on behalf of another. The person appointed to act is the agent; the person appointing the agent is the principal.

agent *see* AGENCY.

agent provocateur a person who incites someone to commit a crime for the purposes of ENTRAPMENT, where the crime would not otherwise have been committed.

age of consent the age (16) at which a female may legally consent to sexual intercourse; for homosexual males, the age of consent is 18.

agnates relatives through the father's side of a family. *See also* COGNATES.

aid or abet or **aid and abet** to help an offender to commit a crime, itself a criminal offence if there is evidence of communication between the parties. The aider or abetter may be tried as an ACCESSORY.

AKA in Scots law, an abbreviation of 'also known as', indicating a person's use of a name other than his or her own. *See also* ALIAS.

alias a name other than his or her own, used by a person in the commission of a crime, to avoid identification and detection. *See also* AKA.

alibi a defence that a person charged with a criminal offence was elsewhere when the offence was committed and therefore cannot be responsible for it.

alien a person who is not a citizen of a state under the terms of the law of that state. In the UK, it applies to anyone who is not a British citizen, a Commonwealth citizen, a British protected person, or a citizen of the Republic of Ireland. Aliens may be designated 'friendly' or 'hostile'.

alienable able to be transferred.

aliment in Scotland, the obligation to maintain a member of one's family. Spouses have such a duty to one another. *See* MAINTENANCE.

alimony a financial provision made by a husband to his separated wife, now called MAINTENANCE.

allegation a statement of fact that must be supported by evidence at a trial.

all risks policy a form of insurance that requires the insured to take all reasonable steps to avoid loss.

alluvio *see* ACCRETION.

alteration a change made in a legal document that may affect its validity. If an alteration is made to a will, it is invalid if not made before execution of the will, or if it cannot be shown to have been executed in the same way as the will.

ambiguity uncertainty of meaning. In legal documents, *patent ambiguity* is clear and obvious; *latent ambiguity* emerges when new information, not contained in the document in question, becomes available.

amendment a change made in a document to correct an error or to make a new claim or ALLEGATION. In the High Court, a writ or pleading may be amended once as a right; the leave of the court is required before any further amendment may be made.

amendment of pleadings alteration or correction of PLEADINGS, which may be effected once without leave of the court before the CLOSE OF PLEADINGS and must be served on the other party. After the close of pleadings, leave is required.

amenity, loss of a result of injury that deprives a person of some 'enjoyment of life'.

amnesty an act that pardons certain, specified past offences.

annuity a sum of money that is paid annually for the lifetime of the beneficiary, who is known as the *annuitant*, or for another specified period.

annulment (1) a court ruling that a marriage was never legally valid. (2) the cancellation of a BANKRUPTCY order on the grounds that the debtor was not bankrupt, or when all debts have been paid.

antecedents the previous criminal record of a person accused of a criminal offence. It may not be offered in evidence unless the crime could only have been committed by a person who had already committed an offence, or if the defendant raises it by denying that he or she has a previous criminal record. Antecedents may be given in a report to aid sentencing.

apology in a LIBEL action, an apology along with a payment made to the court, which may mitigate DAMAGES.

apparent insolvency *see* INSOLVENCY.

appeal the process of taking a case to court in order to have a previous court decision overturned. Appeals are usually heard to determine whether legal errors were made in the original case, rather than to challenge points of fact. The court hearing the appeal is known as the appellate court. *See also* APPELLANT.

appellant a person who takes an APPEAL to an appellate court.

arbiter *see* ARBITRATION.

arbitration the determination of a dispute entrusted to one or more parties other than those involved in the dispute. The arbitrator (known in Scotland as the *arbiter*) must apply the law, but may adopt whatever procedure he or she deems appropriate. Arbitration is commonly used to resolve industrial disputes.

armchair principle a rule applied to the interpretation of the terms of a will when the testator's intention is unclear. It implies that those charged with interpreting the will place themselves in the testator's armchair in an attempt to determine his or her intention.

arraign to open a criminal trial by calling the accused to the bar of the court, establish his or her identity, and to ask whether he or she pleads guilty or not guilty to the charge.

arrears the outstanding part of a debt beyond the date on which repayment was due.

arrest the seizing of a person suspected of an offence. In some circumstances, an arrest WARRANT is required. No warrant is needed if the person arrested is suspected of, or is known to have committed, an ARRESTABLE OFFENCE. *See also* CITIZEN'S ARREST.

arrestable offence an offence for which there is a fixed mandatory sentence or which carries a sentence of five years' imprisonment. Anyone may make an ARREST of a person suspected of such an offence without a WARRANT. Serious arrestable offences include MURDER, TREASON and RAPE.

arrest of judgment a move by an accused person between conviction and sentencing on the grounds that the INDICTMENT was defective.

arson the unlawful destruction by fire of the property of another person, now classified as CRIMINAL DAMAGE, and for which the maximum sentence upon conviction is life imprisonment.

art and part in Scots law, the principle of guilt by association, when the accused can be shown to have acted in concert with another in the commission of a criminal act. *See also* AID OR ABET.

assault an act, other than verbal, that puts another person in fear of immediate physical harm. For a person to be accused of assault, it is not necessary for there to have been physical contact. *See also* BATTERY; INDECENT ASSAULT.

assessment the determining of, e.g. DAMAGES.

assessors persons with special knowledge and expertise who assist a court but do not usually play a part in making decisions.

assignment the transfer of ownership from the assignor to the assignee. If a lease is assigned, the transfer must be by DEED; *equitable assignments* must usually be in writing.

assured tenancy a tenancy agreement that gives the person renting premises SECURITY OF TENURE. Under the terms of the Housing Act 1988, a number of conditions must be met before such an agreement can be made.

assured shorthold tenancy an ASSURED TENANCY granted for a period of not less than six months. The LANDLORD may not determine the tenancy at any time less than six months from the beginning of it.

asylum refuge given by a state to a person subject to an EXTRADITION order by another state. *See also* POLITICAL ASYLUM.

attachment the holding of the property of a debtor until the debt has been paid. The debtor himself or herself may be held.

The most common form of attachment is by making deductions from the debtor's earnings, which are paid by his or her employer to the court.

attempt an act that precedes the uncompleted commission of a crime, and that is itself a criminal act. The most common form is ATTEMPTED MURDER.

attempted murder an act that can only be interpreted as having the objective of committing MURDER.

attendance a sentence imposed on offenders between the ages of 17 and 21. Such offenders are required to spend periods specified by the court at attendance centres, which are non-residential and are administered by local authorities.

attestation the signing of a WILL OR DEED by WITNESSES, who attest that the will or deed has been signed in their presence.

Attorney General the principal LAW OFFICER OF THE CROWN and usually a member of the government. He or she is the government's chief legal adviser and leader of the English bar, and may represent the government in court. In the United States, the Attorney General heads the Department of Justice.

attorney, power of *see* POWER OF ATTORNEY.

auction a method of selling by inviting competing bids. Normally, the item for sale is sold to the person who makes the highest bid.

audit the inspection by independent outside parties of a company's accounts.

autonomy the power of self-government; independence.

autopsy *see* POST-MORTEM.

autrefois acquit literally 'formerly acquitted'. A PLEA IN BAR that an accused has been acquitted on a previous occasion of the offence with which he or she is charged.

autrefois convict literally 'formerly convicted'. A PLEA IN BAR that an accused has been convicted on a previous occasion of the offence with which he or she is charged.

B

bail the releasing from custody of a person awaiting trial or appealing against conviction. Security may be sought and conditions imposed by the court. An undertaking to pay a specified sum of money if the accused fails to attend on the date set for trial may be required from the accused person or from another acting as guarantor. In Scotland, to obtain bail, the accused is required not to commit offences and to inform the court of his or her whereabouts, as well as to appear for trial.

bailiff a court officer employed to seize the property of a debtor and to enforce court orders.

bailment the transfer of goods from one person (the bailor) to another (the bailee) for a specific purpose and without transfer of ownership, such as for the hiring of goods, or the delivery of goods for repair.

balance of probabilities in civil cases, the principle that the case that is more probable should succeed. If neither party presents a more probable case, the burden of proof is vested in the person pursuing the case, and the defender wins.

bankruptcy the condition of a person judged to be insolvent, and the appointing of a TRUSTEE to administer his or her affairs for the benefit of creditors. A bankrupt person may be released from bankruptcy through a DISCHARGE.

banns a public announcement in church of a forthcoming marriage in the Church of England and the Church in Wales. Banns are no longer read in Scotland where notice of the intention to marry must be given to the registrar.

bar (1) a legal impediment. (2) an imaginary barrier in a court of law—only QUEEN'S COUNSEL, court officers and LITIGANTS are permitted to step between the bar and the BENCH.

Bar, The the collective name for BARRISTERS. Persons admitted to the profession by one of the INNS OF COURT are 'called to The Bar'.

bare possibility *see* POSSIBILITY.

bare trust a TRUST that requires the TRUSTEE only to hold the trust property and not to undertake any active duties with regard to it.

barrister a member of The BAR and of one of the INNS OF COURT. Normally, a barrister acts upon the instructions of a SOLICITOR, and presents a case for parties in courts and tribunals. He or she may also write an OPINION. A barrister is also known as COUNSEL. *See also* ADVOCATE.

barter the exchange of goods for other goods rather than for money or other form of payment. In law, some of the same terms apply to barter as apply to sale under the relevant legislation.

battered wife a woman who is physically attacked by her husband. She may apply for a nonmolestation order, which requires her husband not to use violence against her, or an exclusion order, which, for a specified period, excludes her husband from the matrimonial home, even if he is the owner.

battery the use of physical force against a person and against his or her will. *See also* ASSAULT.

bench the seat in a court on which the JUDGE sits. The term is also used to refer to all judges collectively, or a group of judges sitting together.

beneficiary a person who is entitled to ownership of property, most commonly as a result of being named in a WILL.

benefits in kind earnings from employment that do not take the form of wages or salary, such as the use of a company-owned car, medical insurance, etc. They are subject to a different form of taxation from money earnings.

bequest any gift, other than land, made in a WILL.

Beth Din a Jewish court. It deals with matters of Jewish law and has jurisdiction over Jews in matters such as adoption and divorce.

beyond [a] reasonable doubt the standard of proof required in criminal cases. If the PROSECUTION and the DEFENCE have presented equally persuasive cases, the defendant is acquitted. Juries may acquit on the basis of doubt, provided it is genuine.

bigamy the offence of marrying when already married to someone else. A defence is the genuine belief that one's partner is dead, or that the first marriage was annulled.

bill of exchange a written order that requires a person to pay a specified sum of money, by a specified date, to the person writing the order.

bill of indictment a bill that charges a person with an indictable offence, signed by an officer of the court. *See* INDICTMENT.

bill of lading a document that acknowledges transfer of goods conveyed by ship.

bill of rights a document that sets out the rights of citizens and the form of their protection from the state. In the United States, the Bill of Rights comprises the first ten amendments to the Constitution, protecting, for example, freedom of expression and freedom of religious worship.

bill of sale a document that transfers the ownership of goods from one person to another. Usually the transfer is conditional on, for example, the settlement of debt.

bind over order a person to enter into a BOND to guarantee to carry out an act, or not to commit an offence.

blackmail the unwarranted demand with menaces that a person make a form of payment for the personal gain of the blackmailer.

blasphemy insulting or offensive comments, in oral or written form, about the Christian religion.

blight notice a notice requiring a public authority to purchase a property that cannot be sold at full value on the open market because its value is adversely affected by a development plan on the part of the authority.

bond a deed by which a person commits to another to doing something or to refrain from doing something. The person making the commitment is the obligor; the other party is the obligee.

borstal an institution in which young offenders (between the ages of 15 and 20) were held in custody prior to 1983.

breach of confidence disclosing confidential information; failure to obey a court injunction forbidding it. It most commonly applies to sensitive commercial information, and to confidentiality between married partners or cohabitees.

breach of contract failure to fulfil the obligations imposed by the signing of a contract.

breach of the peace behaviour that causes, or is likely to cause, harm to persons or property. In Scotland, conduct that is likely to cause public disturbance, and a more serious offence than in England.

breach of trust the failure of a TRUSTEE to perform the duties stipulated by the terms of a TRUST.

breakdown of marriage the failure of a marriage to the extent that the court will grant a DIVORCE, on the grounds of ADULTERY, UNREASONABLE CONDUCT or DESERTION.

breaking and entering another term for BURGLARY.

bribery and corruption giving or offering a reward to a public servant to act in a particular way in relation to the activities of the body that employs him or her; the offence of receiving such reward.

brief (1) the papers that are given to a BARRISTER in conducting a case. (2) the colloquial term for a barrister.

British citizen since 1983, a person who has the RIGHT OF ABODE in the United Kingdom. Citizenship may be conferred by birth, descent, registration and naturalization. To acquire citizenship by birth, a person must be born in the UK and have one parent who is a UK citizen or is resident in the UK with an unrestricted right to remain under the immigration laws. A person born outside the UK to at least one parent who is a UK citizen acquires citizenship by descent. *See also* BRITISH OVERSEAS CITIZEN; BRITISH PROTECTED PERSON; BRITISH SUBJECT.

British overseas citizen since 1983, a person who did not become a citizen of a former British colony when that colony became independent. Citizenship can be acquired by registration and is most commonly conferred on MINORS.

British protected person a person connected with a former British protectorate, protected state or trust territory who may register as a British citizen by virtue of his or her residence in the UK.

British subject a person who was a citizen of the UK and Colonies as defined by the British Nationality Act 1948, but who did not acquire nationality of his or her country of residence when it became independent or adopted its own nationality laws. Such a person may not be a citizen of any other country (*compare* BRITISH OVERSEAS CITIZEN) and may acquire British citizenship by registration.

brothel premises used for sexual purposes, usually PROSTITUTION. Brothel keeping is an offence. *See also* SOLICITING.

building consent a certificate, issued by a local authority or inspector, that confirms that a planning application conforms with building regulations. In Scotland, the certificate is known as a building warrant.

building warrant *see* BUILDING CONSENT.

burden of proof the onus placed on a LITIGANT to prove certain facts to be true. In criminal cases, the burden of proof rests with the PROSECUTION. *See also* BALANCE OF PROBABILITIES; BEYOND [A] REASONABLE DOUBT.

burglary the offence of entering premises with the purpose of stealing, committing RAPE or GRIEVOUS BODILY HARM, or doing damage. *See also* HOUSEBREAKING.

bye-law a rule drawn up by a body other than Parliament, most commonly a local authority.

C

canon law the law of the Roman Catholic Church and the Church of England.

capacity a person's ability to enter into a legally binding agreement. Those considered incapable of so doing include MINORS, the mentally ill, and the drunk.

capital punishment a form of punishment involving the killing of a person convicted of a crime, colloquially called the 'death penalty'. Capital punishment (by hanging) was abolished in the UK in 1965, though it could still be imposed for high TREASON or PIRACY. In some American states, capital punishment is carried out by use of the electric chair or lethal injection.

careless and inconsiderate driving an offence under the Road Traffic Act 1991 involving the driving of a motor vehicle in a public place without due care and attention.

care order a court order that places a child in the care of a local authority that then has most of the same powers and responsibilities as a parent.

cartel the coming together of a number of commercial enterprises to create a monopoly, usually with the purpose of fixing prices.

causation the connection between an act and the consequences of it. In law, it may be necessary to prove causation before the accused can be convicted of a crime, such as MURDER.

caution an indication, to be given under most circumstances, by a police officer to a person he or she suspects of having committed an offence, which follows a standard form of words. *See* INTERROGATION; RIGHT OF SILENCE.

caveat emptor literally 'let the buyer beware', a warning that the buyer of goods has no claim against the vendor unless he or she has previously sought a guarantee from the vendor that the goods were not defective. This maxim has largely been superceded by consumer protection legislation.

Central Criminal Court the principal CROWN COURT for Central London, popularly known as the 'Old Bailey'.

certification of entitlement proof that a person has RIGHT OF ABODE in the UK if unable to show a British passport or otherwise prove British citizenship.

certiorari originally, a High Court WRIT ordering an inferior court to remove proceedings to a superior court. It may now be used to quash the decisions of a tribunal.

challenge to jury a procedure whereby prosecution or defence may challenge a member of the JURY before they are sworn in.

chambers the room of a JUDGE or the offices of a BARRISTER.

Chancery Division a division of the High Court of Justice, principally concerned with matters relating to property, trusts, estates, company law and patents. *See also* FAMILY DIVISION; QUEEN'S BENCH DIVISION.

character evidence in criminal proceedings, evidence as to the bad character of an accused may only be given if attempts have been made to establish good character; character evidence is not usually relevant in civil cases, except DEFAMATION.

charge (1) the formal accusation that the accused person has committed a specific crime. (2) a legal interest in land.

charter party a written document by which the owner of a ship lets the vessel to a charterer for the carriage of cargo, or undertakes that the vessel will carry a cargo. *See also* LAY DAYS.

chattels a term used to describe property other than freehold land.

chose a thing. A *chose in possession* is something that can be owned; a *chose in action* is a legally enforceable right.

choses in action *see* CHOSE.

cif or **c.i.f. [cost, insurance and freight]** a transaction in which the price of goods quoted by the vendor to the purchaser includes the cost of the goods, freight charges and the cost of insuring the goods in transit. *See also* FOB.

Circuit Court a superior court in the Republic of Ireland.

circuit judge a JUDGE who sits in COUNTY COURTS and the CROWN COURT.

circumstantial evidence indirect evidence of a fact, which a JUDGE and JURY may infer but which is not directly proved. *See also* DIRECT EVIDENCE.

citizen's arrest the ARREST of a person by a member of the public who has witnessed, or believes he or she has witnessed, the arrested person committing a crime. No WARRANT is needed; only reasonable force may be used.

citizenship the relationship between a person and a state that offers the individual certain rights and protection, and imposes certain obligations. *See* BRITISH CITIZEN.

civil contempt *see* CONTEMPT OF COURT.

civil law the law of a nation that relates to private matters and is not CRIMINAL LAW or SERVICE LAW.

claim of privilege *see* PRIVILEGE.

clean break an arrangement between parties to a DIVORCE that formally ends their financial relationship. The spouse with care of a child or children can apply to the Child Support Agency in seeking MAINTENANCE even after a clean break settlement.

client a person who employs the services of a SOLICITOR; as a solicitor's client cannot directly employ a BARRISTER, the solicitor is the barrister's client.

close of pleadings PLEADINGS are deemed closed 14 days after the serving of a REPLY or a defence to counterclaim.

closing speeches the speeches made at the end of a court case before the judge's SUMMING UP. The DEFENCE usually makes the final closing speech.

co-accused in Scotland, a person accused with another of committing a crime.

codicil a document that amends a WILL and must be drawn up in the same way as a will.

cognates relatives through the mother's side of a family. *See also* AGNATES.

cohabitation living together as husband and wife, but without being married. For certain purposes a cohabiting couple are treated as though they were married, provided a number of conditions are met.

collateral (1) descent from a common ancestor but through different lines. (2) additional security for a debt.

collective trespass offences when two or more people are believed guilty of TRESPASS with the intention of living on land that belongs to someone else. All those trespassing may be required to leave if any one has caused damage or used threatening behaviour towards the owner.

Commissioner for Oaths a person appointed by the LORD CHANCELLOR to administer OATHS or take AFFIDAVITS.

committal sending a person for trial or to a term of imprisonment.

common assault a form of ASSAULT, a less serious form than aggravated assault.

common law the law based on 'the common sense of the community', developed by the royal courts between the 11th and 13th centuries to apply to the whole nation and supplant local practice.

Commonwealth citizen a person who is a BRITISH CITIZEN, a British Dependent Territories citizen, a BRITISH OVERSEAS CITIZEN, a BRITISH SUBJECT, or a citizen of an independent Commonwealth country.

Community law the law of the European Union, and superior to the law of member states.

community service order an order that requires an offender to do unpaid work in the community, under the supervision of a PROBATION OFFICER, as an alternative to imprisonment.

company *see* PUBLIC COMPANY.

compellability the power to make a WITNESS come to court and TESTIFY. A number of categories are not compellable, including the sovereign, some diplomats, members of parliament and, in some cases, spouses, though all may give evidence as COMPETENT WITNESSSES.

competent witnesses persons who are deemed capable of giving evidence, and, with some exceptions, taken to include anybody of sound mind and sufficient understanding.

complainant a person who alleges that a crime has been committed. *See also* COMPLAINER.

complainer in Scotland, the person who instigates a criminal investigation.

complaint (1) the initiation of civil proceedings in a MAGISTRATES' COURT, consisting of the statement by a COMPLAINANT. (2) an ALLEGATION made by one person against another. (3) in Scotland, the papers served on the ACCUSED in criminal proceedings.

completion the final stage in the process of selling land when payment is exchanged for the land and its TITLE. *See also* SETTLEMENT.

compounding an offence *see* IMPEDING APPREHENSION.

compulsory purchase the legal acquisition of land for public use, which does not take account of the wishes of the owners.

concealment *see* NON-DISCLOSURE.

conciliation the settling of a dispute outside court and often with the help of a disinterested third party.

conclusive evidence evidence that is not open to dispute and which, in law, must be taken to establish a fact.

concurrent sentence a sentence of imprisonment that runs at the same time as another sentence. *See also* CONSECUTIVE SENTENCE.

concurrent tortfeasors *see* JOINT TORTFEASORS.

conditional discharge *see* DISCHARGE.

confession an admission of guilt made by a person accused of a crime. The PROSECUTION is required to prove beyond reasonable doubt that a confession was made voluntarily and not under duress or threat.

conflict of laws *see* PRIVATE INTERNATIONAL LAW.

consanguinity the blood relationship resulting from descent from a common ancestor. *See also* AFFINITY.

consecutive sentence a sentence of imprisonment that follows another sentence. *See also* CONCURRENT SENTENCE.

consideration an exchange of promises between parties making a CONTRACT, by which one party buys the promise of the other.

conspiracy an agreement, which is itself a criminal offence, between two or more persons that one of them will commit an offence. Spouses cannot be guilty of conspiracy.

constitutional law the law relating to the relationship between a citizen and the state, which controls the activities of the different branches of the state.

constructive notice *see* NOTICE.

consumer protection the body of laws that protect the rights of those who purchase goods or services from others. These particular laws do not apply when purchaser and vendor are both in a business relationship. They require the vendor to show that he or she has the right to sell the goods, that the goods fit any description of them, and that they are of merchantable quality and fit for their purpose. Some legislation also covers the safety of goods.

consummation full sexual intercourse between married partners. Failure to consummate a marriage may be grounds for ANNULMENT.

contempt of court behaviour that fails to show due respect to the court. *Criminal contempt* is conduct that obstructs the administration of justice; *civil contempt* is a failure to obey a court order. Both are punishable offences.

contingency fee a fee for legal services that is payable only if the services bought are successful.

contract an agreement that is legally binding, provided a number of conditions are met. Unless the contract is made by DEED, there must be CONSIDERATION; the parties must be free to make the agreement; and the contract must comply with any legal requirements.

contributory negligence lack of care for his or her own safety on the part of a PLAINTIFF. DAMAGES may be reduced if the plaintiff is shown to be partly at fault.

conveyancing the process by which the ownership of property is transferred. When goods are bought, CONSUMER PROTECTION legislation usually covers the conveyancing; conveyancing as it relates to the transfer of ownership in land is usually carried out by SOLICITORS.

conviction finding a person guilty of an offence.

cooling-off period a specified time during which a person may withdraw from a legally binding CONTRACT without heavy penalty.

copyright the right of a person to protection of created work, such as literature, paintings, photographs, etc, from copying or unauthorized use. Generally, the term of copyright is 70 years from the death of the author of the work.

co-respondent a person who is accused of having sexual intercourse with the married partner of someone else. ADULTERY may be a ground for DIVORCE. Such a person must be named in a divorce petition before being a party to divorce proceedings.

coroner a person appointed by the Crown to investigate deaths by ordering a post mortem or an INQUEST.

corporal punishment a form of punishment that is inflicted on the body. *See also* CAPITAL PUNISHMENT.

corporate personality *see* PERSONALITY.

corroboration EVIDENCE that confirms the accuracy of other evidence, e.g. by being given by two independent sources.

corrupt and illegal practices in the conduct of elections, the use of bribery or intimidation, etc, is a corrupt practice; spending more on a political campaign than is legally permitted is an illegal practice.

cost, insurance and freight *see* CIF.

costs legal expenses incurred in the course of an action. They are usually awarded to the winner and against the loser.

counsel another term for an ADVOCATE or a BARRISTER, sometimes used to refer to barristers generally. *See* QUEEN'S COUNSEL.

count *see* INDICTMENT.

counterfeiting the offence of illegally copying coins or notes of a currency with the intention of presenting them as genuine.

County Court a civil court in England and Wales. Each court has a CIRCUIT JUDGE. *See also* HIGH COURT.

court martial a court that tries cases of SERVICE LAW.

Court of Appeal the court that hears appeals against judgments in England and Wales. The civil division, which hears appeals from the HIGH COURT and the COUNTY COURT, is headed by the MASTER OF THE ROLLS, and the criminal division, hearing appeals from the CROWN COURT, by the LORD CHIEF JUSTICE.

Court of Chivalry an ancient feudal court that decided disputes on such matters as the right to bear coats of arms.

Court of Justice the principal court of the European Union. It is charged with ensuring that the law is observed in the interpretation and application of the various treaties agreed by the member states.

Court of Session the highest civil court in Scotland. Appeals held by its Inner House can go to further appeal in the House of Lords.

covenant an agreement contained in a CONTRACT or a DEED. *See also* RESTRICTIVE COVENANT.

crime an action, or a failure to act, which is an offence and which can be punished by the state.

criminal contempt *see* CONTEMPT OF COURT.

criminal court a court that tries criminal, rather than civil, cases.

criminal damage unlawfully damaging or destroying someone else's property. The offence is *aggravated criminal damage* if someone's life is put at risk.

criminal law the law of a nation that deals with the definition of OFFENCES and the punishment of OFFENDERS.

criminal negligence the degree of NEGLIGENCE that establishes liability for a criminal offence. *See also* CONTRIBUTORY NEGLIGENCE.

cross-examination the questioning of a WITNESS by someone other than the person who called the witness to give evidence. *See* LEADING QUESTION.

Crown Court in England and Wales, part of the SUPREME COURT. It hears criminal cases and may hear appeals from MAGISTRATES' COURTS. Although one court, it sits in different parts of the country.

Crown Prosecution Service a government agency that prosecutes criminal cases in England. It is headed by the Director of Public Prosecutions. In Scotland, the equivalent agency is the Procurator Fiscal.

culpable homicide in Scotland, unlawful killing that is not defined as MURDER. It also covers cases where recklessness or gross negligence in the course of a legal activity has caused death. *See also* MANSLAUGHTER.

custody (1) holding a person in imprisonment or confinement. (2) legal possession or control. Under acts in England in 1989 and Scotland in 1995, the custody of children was redefined as a part of parental responsibility.

D

damages a sum awarded by a court to a victim of BREACH OF CONTRACT to compensate a loss. The type and level vary: NOMINAL DAMAGES may be awarded if no actual damage has been caused, e.g. to reputation or financial status; SUBSTANTIAL DAMAGES may be awarded when there has been actual damage; EXEMPLARY DAMAGES may be awarded to punish the defendant.

dangerous driving the offence, formerly called reckless driving, of driving a motor vehicle in a manner that causes or is likely to cause death or injury to a person, or damage to property.

data protection various forms of protection of personal information about individuals, which is gathered and stored in computer files.

death penalty *see* CAPITAL PUNISHMENT.

debenture a document that acknowledges a DEBT owed by a company and specifies the interest rate payable and the term of the debt.

debt (1) a sum of money owed by one party to another. (2) the obligation to pay the sum owed.

deceit knowingly or recklessly making a false statement with the intention that another party act on the information given and suffer loss thereby. *See also* FRAUD.

deception acting or speaking, or intending to act or speak, so as falsely to represent a fact. Deception is not a criminal offence, but there are a number of punishable crimes that involve deception, including obtaining an overdraft or insurance policy by deception, and purchasing property by deception.

decree an order made by a court. A *decree nisi* conditionally terminates a marriage; a *decree absolute* fully terminates the marriage and leaves the partners free to remarry.

deed a written document that must be signed by the person making it in the presence of a WITNESS. Prior to 1990, to be valid, a deed had to be literally 'signed, sealed and delivered'.

deed poll a DEED to which there is only one party, used, for example, legally to change one's name.

defamation publishing in words or pictures a statement about a person that has the effect of diminishing his or her reputation. The distinction in English law between LIBEL and SLANDER is not observed in Scotland.

default failure to do something that the law requires should be done, such as repaying a loan. In court proceedings, if a party fails to take certain clearly laid down steps, a judgment in default may be made.

defect a fault, usually in goods that have been bought. An obvious fault is known as a *patent defect*; a fault that is not obvious is a *latent defect*. The latter affords the purchaser legal remedy against the vendor; the former usually does not if the goods could have been inspected prior to purchase.

defence (1) the plea made by a DEFENDANT in court. (2) a legal or factual issue that, if given in favour of the defendant, absolves him or her. (3) the colloquial name for the COUNSEL acting for the defendant. In criminal trials defence consists in a NOT GUILTY plea.

defendant a person against whom court proceedings are brought.

deferred sentence in Scotland, the postponing for a long or short period of the SENTENCING of an offender. *See also* SUSPENDED SENTENCE.

delegated legislation largely governmental law-making under powers conferred by Acts of Parliament. *See also* BYE-LAW; ORDERS OF COUNCIL.

delegation assigning a duty to another person; granting another person the authority to act on behalf of the grantor.
delict in Scots law, civil LIABILITY. *See also* TORT.
demanding with menaces a form of BLACKMAIL.
dependant a person who depends on another or others for maintenance. The term usually applies to a spouse or former spouse, and children. Provision may be made by the state from the ESTATE of a deceased person to continue financial support.
dependent territory a territory or colony whose government is to a greater or lesser extent the responsibility of another state. *See also* BRITISH CITIZEN.
deportation the expulsion from the United Kingdom of a person who has broken the conditions of permission to stay; a member of whose family is deported; who is convicted of an offence punishable by imprisonment; or whose removal is deemed to be for the public good.
deposition a statement made by a WITNESS under OATH, and recorded in writing.
deprave and corrupt *see* OBSCENE PUBLICATIONS.
derogation in European Community law, exemption from some aspects of legislation.
descent the transmission of citizenship from one generation to another. British citizenship may be transmitted by either parent.
desertion the ending by one partner, without the consent or agreement of the other, of a COHABITATION arrangement. It usually, but not necessarily, involves the deserting partner leaving the shared home. As a valid ground for DIVORCE, desertion must be followed by two years' continuous non-cohabitation.
detention holding a person against his or her will. Although usually an offence, it is authorised in certain circumstances, e.g. the holding of a person arriving in the UK in anticipation of a removal or DEPORTATION order.

devise a gift by WILL of REAL PROPERTY, such as an interest in LAND. *See also* LEGACY; PERSONAL PROPERTY.

devolution (1) the legal transfer of property from one person to another. (2) in CONSTITUTIONAL LAW, the granting of some powers to an inferior body, such as a local authority, a regional government or an assembly.

digest a compilation of laws; a collection of case SUMMARIES.

diminished responsibility a DEFENCE in MITIGATION to a charge of MURDER on the grounds that the DEFENDANT was not certifiably insane but was temporarily of diminished mental capacity.

Din Torah in Jewish law, the hearing of a case before the BETH DIN.

diplomatic immunity freedom from legal proceedings against members of diplomatic missions to the Court of St James, i.e. to the UK. The level of immunity varies according to the diplomatic staff member's status and rank.

direct evidence a statement made by a WITNESS in court to support facts given; a statement by a witness that he or she observed a fact through the use of one of his or her own senses. *See also* CIRCUMSTANTIAL EVIDENCE; HEARSAY EVIDENCE.

Director of Public Prosecutions the head of the CROWN PROSECUTION SERVICE, responsible for preparing all cases instituted by the police.

Disability Discrimination Act a law prohibiting unjustifiable discrimination against anyone with a disability in employment or in the provision of goods and services, which took effect in the UK in 1996.

discharge (1) the termination of an agreement and any obligations that go with it. (2) the release without punishment of a convicted person—an *absolute discharge* confers freedom; a *conditional discharge* requires the released person not to be convicted of another offence during a stipulated period.

disclaimer (1) a refusal to act, e.g. as the beneficiary under the terms of a WILL. (2) a move by a person to limit LIABILITY attaching to him or her.

discovery and inspection of documents in civil LITIGATION, the disclosure to the opposing party of relevant documents in an action.

discrimination treatment, which may be illegal, of an individual or group in a manner that is less favourable than that applied to other individuals or groups. *See* RACIAL DISCRIMINATION; SEX DISCRIMINATION.

dishonour of a bill of exchange failure to honour a BILL OF EXCHANGE, either by non-acceptance or non-payment.

disorderly house another term for a BROTHEL.

disqualification depriving a person of a right. A driver may be disqualified from driving as a penalty for committing a motoring offence; a company director may be disqualified for fraudulent trading.

divorce the legal ending of a marriage, other than by ANNULMENT. The ground for divorce is irretrievable BREAKDOWN OF MARRIAGE and may be occasioned by ADULTERY, DESERTION, UNREASONABLE CONDUCT or SEPARATION.

DNA fingerprinting *see* GENETIC FINGERPRINTING.

D notice a request to newspaper editors and broadcasters not to publish or broadcast information that might damage national security, which may or may not be covered by the OFFICIAL SECRETS Act.

documentary evidence evidence that is written rather than spoken. To be admissible, the document has to be shown to be authentic and that it performs a proper purpose. *See also* HEARSAY EVIDENCE.

domicile the country that a person treats as his or her permanent home. A *domicile of origin* is acquired at birth, through the father first, then if he is dead, through the mother. A *domicile of* *choice* may be acquired later (after the age of 16) by making another place one's permanent home. A person may have only one domicile at any time.

dominant tenement *see* EASEMENT.

donatio mortis causa a gift of property made by a person who expects to die. The property must be capable of being a gift; death must be anticipated, and the gift must be capable of being delivered.

double jeopardy the rule that a person may not be prosecuted twice for the same crime. Such a person may, however, be prosecuted for a different offence, such as PERJURY.

drunk driving an offence that involves driving or being in charge of a motor vehicle while unfit through alcohol or drugs.

due process of law the legal system functioning properly, which protects individuals from arbitrary justice.

duress pressure exerted on a person to act in a particular way. *See also* CONFESSION.

duty of care (1) a legal obligation to avoid causing damage to persons or property. (2) the responsibility on people who handle waste and waste products to dispose of it safely. *See also* NEGLIGENCE.

dying declaration the oral or writen evidence of a dying person given at the trial of a person accused of his or her MURDER.

E

easement a right enjoyed by an owner of land that confers rights over neighbouring land owned by another person. The land owned is known as the *dominant tenement*; the other land as the *servient tenement*.

easement of light a right to enjoy uninterrupted light from a window without obstruction for 20 years.

ecclesiastical court a court that administers the ecclesiastical law of the Church of England.

EC law *see* COMMUNITY LAW.

economic loss loss suffered by a plaintiff through negligence. The loss is usually financial rather than physical or proprietary.

edictal citation in Scotland, serving court papers in pursuit of a civil action by posting them on the walls of a court because the defendant cannot be traced and the papers cannot therefore be served on him or her.

ejection in Scotland, an action to remove a person from a piece of land.

ejusdem generis the rule that a list of things in statutes must be taken to be of one type or classification.

election the principle that a person must accept both benefits and burdens conferred under the terms of a WILL, or reject both.

electronic surveillance the interception of communications through the use of hidden microphones, 'phone tapping', etc. EVIDENCE obtained using such methods is usually admissible.

embezzlement until 1968, the appropriation by an employee of property acquired on behalf of his or her employer, now a form of THEFT.

emblements crops that are harvested annually. Despite loss of rights over land, a tenant may continue to enjoy the benefit of sown crops.

emergency powers special powers conferred by royal proclamation on government during a state of emergency.

emergency protection order a court order that gives a local authority or other body the right to remove to its protection a child at risk of harm. Also known as a place of safety order.

emoluments a person's earnings from employment, and including perquisites and profits. *See also* BENEFITS IN KIND.

empanel to swear in a JURY to hear a case.

employee a person who works under the direction of another person in exchange for payment.

employer a person who engages another person to work under his or her direction in exchange for payment.

Employment Appeal Tribunal a statutory body that hears appeals from INDUSTRIAL TRIBUNALS.

encroachment unlawful interference with the rights of, or land belonging to, another person.

encumbrance an interest in land held by someone other than the owner of the land, e.g. a MORTGAGE.

endorsement (1) the details of a motoring conviction as marked on a driving licence (*see* TOTTING UP). (2) the signature of a holder on a BILL OF EXCHANGE. (3) details on a document of a transaction that affects the contents of the document.

endowment property that belongs to a charitable organisation; a commitment to giving a fixed sum to a charity.

enduring power of attorney *see* POWER OF ATTORNEY.

enforcement notice the requirement by a local planning authority that steps be taken within a specified period to rectify a breach of planning regulations.

enforcement of judgment the enforcement of a court order, e.g. the payment of a FINE.

enfranchise (1) to confer the right to vote in an election. (2) to give a person or group the right to be represented.

engagement an agreement to marry, unenforceable in law. In Scotland, prior to 1984, an engagement was a legally binding CONTRACT.

engross to prepare a final fair copy of a DEED or other legal document.

entailed interest an interest in land granted to a person and his or her heirs only.

enter judgment in civil actions, to record formally a court judgment.

enticement in Scotland, luring a person away from his or her family.

entitled spouse in Scotland, a person who owns or rents a house, or has some other entitlement to live in it. The non-entitled spouse can obtain an EXCLUSION ORDER.

entrapment encouraging a person to commit an offence with the aim of securing a conviction. Entrapment may not be used as a defence as the defendant is assumed to have been free not to commit the offence, but it may be grounds for MITIGATION.

environmental legislation laws that are designed to enhance the quality of the living environment, or to reduce damage to it from, for example, harmful emissions.

Equal Opportunities Commission a body charged with ending discrimination, principally in employment, on the grounds of sex or marital status. *See* SEX DISCRIMINATION.

equal pay the principle that men and women should be equally rewarded for the same work. *See* SEX DISCRIMINATION.

equitable in accord with the rules of EQUITY; just and fair.

equity (1) a body of law designed to remedy disputes that could not be heard under common law. (2) a share in a LIMITED COMPANY.

equity of redemption the right of a mortgagor to redeem property during the term of a MORTGAGE.

error a mistake made by a court in passing judgment. The practice of referring an error to a superior court has been abolished and replaced by the APPEAL system.

escape the offence of unlawfully escaping from CUSTODY. It is also an offence to help a person being lawfully held to escape.

escrow a DEED that is given to a third party, often a SOLICITOR, to hold until all conditions of the deed have been fulfilled.

estate ownership of LAND; all property to which a person is beneficially entitled.

estate duty until 1975, a tax that was levied on the value of property owned by a deceased person. *See* INHERITANCE TAX.

estoppel a rule that prevents a person from denying the truth of a statement he or she has made or from denying facts alleged, when the statement has been acted on, usually to his or her disadvantage, by another party. A *promissory estoppel* applies when one party promises not to enforce his or her rights under a contract. A *proprietary estoppel* is a doctrine under which the court can grant a REMEDY when an owner of land has led another to act detrimentally in the belief that rights over land would be acquired.

European Commission on Human Rights the body in the EUROPEAN COURT OF HUMAN RIGHTS that receives complaints from individuals or states regarding breaches of the EUROPEAN CONVENTION ON HUMAN RIGHTS.

European Convention on Human Rights an acceptance by members of the European Union that citizens should enjoy HUMAN RIGHTS. Specific freedoms are stipulated: the right to life; freedom from torture; freedom from slavery; the right to liberty unless held in accordance with the law; the right to justice; the right to privacy; the right to peaceful assembly; freedom from discrimination. Further rights are added from time to time.

European Court of Human Rights a chamber of judges that hears cases under the terms of the EUROPEAN CONVENTION ON HUMAN RIGHTS.

euthanasia the unlawful killing (sometimes called 'mercy killing') of a terminally ill person in accordance with that person's wishes.

eviction (1) the recovery of land by due process of law. (2) the removal of a person from possession of property.

evidence that which may or may not be brought before a court to establish the existence or non-existence of a fact; loosely used to describe facts presented during the course of an action. Evidence can take a number of different forms. *See* CIRCUM-

STANTIAL EVIDENCE; DIRECT EVIDENCE; DOCUMENTARY EVIDENCE; HEARSAY EVIDENCE; INSUFFICIENT EVIDENCE.

evidence obtained illegally EVIDENCE that has been obtained in contravention of a law. It may be ruled inadmissible on the grounds of fairness.

evidential burden the requirement to prove the truth of something. *See also* BALANCE OF PROBABILITIES; BURDEN OF PROOF.

examination the questioning of a WITNESS under OATH.

examination in chief the questioning of a WITNESS by the party who called him or her to give EVIDENCE. LEADING QUESTIONS are not allowed. *See also* CROSS EXAMINATION; RE-EXAMINATION.

exchange of contracts in property purchase, the exchange between purchaser and seller of identical signed copies of the contract of sale, at which point the transaction is legally binding.

exchange of pleadings a process by which a plaintiff's statement of claim is given to the defendant, the defence to the plaintiff and the plaintiff's reply to the defendant.

excise tax (1) tax charged on the retail sale of beer, wines, spirits, etc. (2) certain types of licence, e.g. to use a gun. (3) the licence that must be displayed on motor vehicles in public places.

exclusionary rule in rules of EVIDENCE, the rule which allows the court to exclude evidence which is technically admissible, but which is considered prejudicial.

exclusion order (1) the exclusion from the UK of a person under the terms of the Prevention of Terrorism Act. Such an order can also be used to exclude a person convicted of other offences, such as drug trafficking. (2) a court order excluding a spouse from the matrimonial home for the protection of the other spouse or a child.

excusable homicide the killing of a person in SELF-DEFENCE or by an accident which does not involve NEGLIGENCE.

executed trust a TRUST in which the settlor has declared the limitations of the estate of the trustees and beneficiaries such that no further instrument is needed to define those interests.

execution (1) the signing of a DEED or other document to make it legally valid. (2) carrying out a court order. (3) the fulfilling of the terms of a CONTRACT.

executor a person named in a WILL who accepts responsibility for the administration of the testator's ESTATE. Unlike a WITNESS, an executor may be a BENEFICIARY of a will.

exemplary damages or **punitive damages** DAMAGES awarded to punish the defendant as well as to compensate the plaintiff.

exemption clause a term in a CONTRACT that excuses a person from liability under the terms of the contract, or from some other obligation. It is important that such a clause genuinely form part of the contract and be unambiguous.

ex gratia as a favour and without legal obligation, as in an *ex gratia* payment.

exhibit an object or document, identified by letter or number, and shown in court to a WITNESS and to the JURY, or mentioned in an AFFIDAVIT.

exhumation the digging up of a body that has been buried.

existing goods goods which are the subject of a contract of sale and which the vendor already owns. *See also* FUTURE GOODS.

ex officio by virtue of an office held. The LORD CHANCELLOR is, *ex officio*, a member of the government.

ex parte on behalf of. A court may rely on a statement made on behalf of a person during an *ex parte* hearing.

***ex parte* inspection order** a court order that documents may be seen without the consent or knowledge of the owner of the documents in circumstances where it is held that the owner may try to prevent the documents being seen.

expert witness a WITNESS who is permitted to express an opinion when giving EVIDENCE, on the understanding that he or she has expert or specialist knowledge that other parties do not have.

expropriation the taking by the state of private property for public use and without a requirement to pay COMPENSATION. *See also* COMPULSORY PURCHASE.

extended sentence a sentence that is longer than the MAXIMUM SENTENCE for a specific offence. Circumstances in which it may be imposed include persistent offending, and committing an offence within a specified period following a previous conviction.

extortion (1) using physical force to obtain something. (2) obtaining something not due through the use of public office. (3) in Scotland, using force to obtain money. *See also* BLACKMAIL.

extradition the surrender by one country to another of a person who is accused of committing an offence in the second country. For the procedure to operate from the UK, there must be an extradition treaty between the UK and the country requesting extradition, and other conditions must also be met.

extraordinary general meeting a specially arranged meeting of the members or owners of a company which, unlike an annual general meeting, is only called to discuss special business.

F

fact something that is known or can be shown to exist or to have happened.

factor an agent to whom goods are entrusted with the aim of selling them. *See also* MERCANTILE AGENT.

Faculty of Advocates in Scotland, the college of ADVOCATES headed by the dean. It is responsible for its members' conduct

failure to maintain the failure of a spouse to make adequate provision for the other spouse or for children of the marriage.

fair comment a defence to an action for DEFAMATION that the assertion was based on true facts and that the comment or opinion expressed was fair and in the public interest.

fair dismissal the dismissal of a person from a post judged by a TRIBUNAL to have been reasonable and lawful. *See also* UNFAIR DISMISSAL.

fair rent a RENT that is determined by a rent officer or a committee and is intended to be fair in view of the position, age, state of repair, degree of furnishings, etc. of a property, and not based on the personal circumstances of the rentor.

fair wear and tear the principle that a TENANT, though not necessarily responsible for general repairs to a property, should nevertheless take all reasonable steps to ensure that the property is maintained in a good state of repair.

false accounting the offence of falsifying, concealing or destroying a document which is used in the accounting process in order to gain for onself or cause loss to another party.

false imprisonment the unlawful and unauthorised holding of a person against his or her will.

false instrument a document, stamp, recording, etc. which purports to have been made in its present form by a person who did not make it in that form. *See also* FORGERY.

Family Division a division of the High Court of Justice concerned with family proceedings. *See also* CHANCERY DIVISION; QUEEN'S BENCH DIVISION.

fee simple absolute in possession a form of land ownership that does not end on death and is unconditional.

felony an obsolete term for an offence that is more serious than a MISDEMEANOUR.

fence the colloquial term for a person who receives stolen goods. *See* HANDLING; RESET.

fiction the assumption that something is true, whether it really is true or not.

fiduciary relationship a relationship based on trust in which one person (such as a TRUSTEE) is under an obligation to act solely for the benefit of another person.

final judgment in civil proceedings, the court JUDGMENT that brings an action to an end. *See also* INTERLOCUTORY JUDGMENT.

financial provision in Scotland, the payment of a sum or periodical allowance, or the transfer of property on DIVORCE.

financial relief any of a number of orders that relate to MAINTENANCE pending a petition for DIVORCE. The court has the power to set aside any agreement made between husband and wife.

fine a sum of money payable by an offender on conviction. The court will take into account the financial circumstances of the offender and the seriousness of the offence in determining the amount of the fine according to a scale that sets maximums.

firearm a barrelled weapon from which a shot, bullet or missile can be fired and which is potentially lethal. The term also describes any prohibited weapon even if not lethal.

fire-raising in Scotland, the criminal offence of recklessly setting a fire, or the intention of so doing. *See also* ARSON.

first instance the first court hearing of a case.

first offender a person before a court who has no previous criminal conviction. A first offender usually escapes imprisonment unless the court finds it is the only appropriate sentence.

fishing interrogatory an INTERROGATORY that has no specific reference and is made in the hope that some matter will emerge. Normally such orders are not granted by the courts.

fitness for purpose an implied condition that must be met by someone selling goods, which have a specified purpose, to another.

fixed charge an interest attached to an item of property such as land. *See also* FLOATING CHARGE.

fixed penalty notice a notice offering an offender the opportunity to pay a FINE, which will discharge any liability and avoid prosecution. The offender may choose not to pay and elect to be prosecuted for the offence.

fixed term a LEASE that stipulates an agreed period of TENANCY.

fixture something that is attached to a building or to land and is taken to be part of it. Interpretation as to what constitutes a fixture varies and can lead to disputes. Two criteria often used are how easily or otherwise a fixture might be moved; and the extent of likely damage caused by moving it.

flagrante delicto in the course of committing an offence. The term is most frequently used in relation to an accusation of ADULTERY. *See* PROVOCATION.

floating charge an interest attached to items such as cash or stock in trade. *See also* FIXED CHARGE.

flotation the process of raising capital to finance a business. It usually involves an invitation, directly or indirectly, to the public to acquire shares in the company.

flying picket a person who appears on a picket line to support those involved in an industrial dispute but is not directly involved in the dispute. *See* PICKETING.

fob or **f.o.b. (free on board)** a transaction in which the purchaser of goods bears the cost of insuring the goods in transit as well as their price and the cost of freight. *See also* CIF.

footpath a HIGHWAY over which members of the public have RIGHT OF WAY on foot. *See also* FOOTWAY.

footway a way over which members of the public have RIGHT OF WAY on foot and which may also be used by vehicular traffic.

forbearance deliberate failure to exercise a legal right.

force majeure an event which could not have been anticipated and which cannot be controlled.

forcible entry gaining entry to premises by force. It is an offence if someone is present on the premises and opposes the entry. Ownership of the property entered is only a defence in certain circumstances.

foreclosure the right of a mortgagee to claim ownership of property to satisfy an unpaid debt (usually a MORTGAGE). Foreclosure must be by the granting of a court order.

foreign judgment a judgment made by a court in another country that, if a number of specific conditions are met, can be enforced in the UK.

foresight an awareness that an act will have certain consequences. It can be sufficient to confer liability, although INTENTION may also have to be established.

forfeiture the loss of property or a right through the failure of the holder to fulfil an obligation. A person with a superior interest may end the holding of an inferior interest, e.g. a tenant's lease.

forgery (1) the offence of making a FALSE INSTRUMENT and passing it off as genuine to deceive another person who incurs a loss. (2) the counterfeiting of currency.

formal contract a CONTRACT for the sale of land which lists details of the property and any special conditions relating to the sale. *See* OPEN CONTRACT.

forum (1) the place where a case is heard. (2) also refers to the legal system that has JURISDICTION.

foster parents those who look after a child who is not their own by blood or ADOPTION. Foster parents have no legal rights over such a child, but can apply to have the child made a WARD of court.

Four Freedoms in the laws of the European Union, four freedoms that were enshrined in the Treaty that set up the Common Market. *See* FREEDOM OF ESTABLISHMENT; FREE MOVEMENT OF CAPITAL; FREE MOVEMENT OF GOODS; FREE MOVEMENT OF PERSONS.

franchise (1) the right to vote in an election. (2) the granting by one trader to another of the grantor's expertise and the good will of his or her business in return for some form of payment, often a fee or commission.

fraud false representation to achieve a practical gain, which may or may not be financial. In Scotland, false representation made in the knowledge that it is untrue and with the intention that another party rely in the statement made and so incur a loss. *See also* DECEIT.

fraudulent misrepresentation *see* MISREPRESENTATION.

fraudulent trading conducting business transactions for a fraudulent purpose or to defraud creditors.

freedom of establishment one of the FOUR FREEDOMS; the right of a person to pursue his or her profession or vocation as a self-employed person in another EU member state.

free movement of capital one of the FOUR FREEDOMS; the right of residents of EU member countries to move capital regardless of their nationality or where the capital is invested.

free movement of goods one of the FOUR FREEDOMS; the removal of barriers to the movement of goods for trade between member states of the EU.

free movement of persons one of the FOUR FREEDOMS; the right of people to move between EU member countries.

freehold the most complete form of ownership of land. *See* FEE SIMPLE ABSOLUTE IN POSSESSION.

freeing for adoption consenting to the ADOPTION of one's own child or children.

free on board *see* FOB.

frustration of contract the termination of a CONTRACT due to unforeseen circumstances that make the purpose of the agreement impossible to achieve or render it illegal.

fugitive offender a person accused in the UK of committing an offence in a Commonwealth country or a British dependent territory. No treaty need exist between the UK and the state involved. *See also* EXTRADITION.

future goods goods that will be made or acquired by the vendor after a contract of sale has been made. *See also* EXISTING GOODS.

future interest a property right that does not take immediate effect.

G

garnishee proceedings a type of execution on debts under which a creditor may obtain a court order for the repayment of a debt against a third party who owes money to, or holds funds on behalf of, the debtor (the garnishee).

gazumping the withdrawal of a vendor in the sale of land in the expectation of a higher offer from another party when the terms of the sale have been agreed but before EXCHANGE OF CONTRACTS. In Scotland, the formal acceptance of an offer to purchase is, subject to certain conditions, legally binding.

GBH *see* GRIEVOUS BODILY HARM.

general damages the DAMAGES that are awarded to compensate for the natural consequence of a TORT, such as loss of reputation in a LIBEL action, which does not need to be proved; the damages awarded for a loss that cannot be exactly calculated or quantified, such as PAIN AND SUFFERING. *See also* SPECIAL DAMAGES.

general defences forms of DEFENCE that relate to INVOLUNTARY CONDUCT. *See also* SPECIAL DEFENCES.

general safety requirement under the Consumer Protection Act 1987, the standard of safety that consumer goods must meet. It is an offence to supply goods that do not meet this standard.

general verdict in civil cases, a VERDICT that is totally in favour of one party or the other; in criminal cases, a verdict of guilty or not guilty. *See also* SPECIAL VERDICT.

genetic fingerprinting or **DNA fingerprinting** the drawing up of an individual's unique genetic profile from cells extracted from tissue. It has most frequently been used in RAPE and PATERNITY cases.

genocide the crime of aiming to destroy through killing or seriously injuring a national, ethnic, racial or religious group.

Ghet a Jewish religious DIVORCE, conducted by the BETH DIN. The husband serves a handwritten bill of divorce on his wife before two witnesses. As the Beth Din administers only religious law, a civil divorce may also be required.

gift the voluntary transfer of property. The transfer of land requires a DEED. A gift by WILL is effective on the death of the testator.

good behaviour in SENTENCING, the requirement that a person should keep the peace and be 'of good behaviour'. *See also* RECOGNIZANCE.

good faith honesty and decency, which can be a requirement in law.

goods (1) personal property excluding land. (2) items offered for sale. *See* FREE MOVEMENT OF GOODS.

goodwill the advantage of a business in the form of the patronage it receives from its customers, and which it can reasonably expect to continue to receive. In the sale of a business as a going concern, goodwill can constitute a substantial part of the value of the business. Protection of it can be sought by requiring the vendor not to set up a rival business which would enjoy patronage from the same customers.

grant the creation or transfer of ownership of property, such as a lease in land. The grant creates an inferior interest with the superior interest retained by the grantor.

Gray's Inn one of the INNS OF COURT in Holborn in London. It is believed to date from the late 14th century.

green form *see* LEGAL AID.

grievous bodily harm (GBH) the criminal offence of intentionally causing serious injury to someone. *See also* ASSAULT; WOUNDING WITH INTENT.

gross indecency a sexual act that does not involve intercourse and is an offence if committed by a man with another man, unless both parties are over the age of 18, consent, and the act is carried out in private; or, if committed with a child under the age of 14. *See also* INDECENCY.

gross negligence a substantial degree of NEGLIGENCE, a breach of a duty of care.

ground rent rent reserved under a long-term LEASE of land and payable by the LESSEE.

group action a court procedure in which a number of claims arising out of the same event, or made against the same defendant, are heard together, e.g. when victims of a rail or air accident sue for DAMAGES.

guarantee (1) an agreement that makes the guarantor responsible for another person's debt. It is a secondary obligation, which only becomes operative if the principal debtor is in default. (2) colloquially, an undertaking given by a manufacturer that it will repair or replace faulty goods for a specified period.

guardian a person who is appointed to take care of a child and assume PARENTAL RESPONSIBILITY. The appointment can be made by court order or privately (when it must be in writing, dated and signed).

guardian *ad litem* a person appointed to represent the interests of a MINOR in court proceedings. If the child has a GUARDIAN, that is usually the person appointed.

guillotine a means of speeding the passing of legislation through Parliament by limiting the time allowed for its various stages.

guilty (1) a plea made in court by the ACCUSED that he or she committed the offence charged. (2) a VERDICT that finds that the accused committed the offence or offences with which he or she is charged. *See also* NOT GUILTY.

H

habeas corpus a WRIT that means literally 'that you have the body' and is used to challenge the holding of a person in CUSTODY. If the custodian fails to appear to justify the detention, the court orders the person held to be released.

habitual criminal an alternative term for a PERSISTENT OFFENDER.

habitual residence the country or place where a person has his or her home. *See also* DOMICILE.

hacking the offence of gaining unauthorized access to computer files. It is also an offence to gain such access in order to steal, alter or destroy stored information, or to breach COPYRIGHT.

Hague Conventions a series of international conventions on the conduct of war. There were three in 1899 and 13 in 1907.

half blood the blood relationship between people who share one ancestor. *See* CONSANGUINITY.

handling [stolen goods] the crime of receiving, retaining or disposing of goods which are known or believed to have been stolen. *See also* RESET.

harassment (1) the use of threatening or abusive words within someone's hearing. (2) threatening a person with distress or humiliation in pursuit of payment or to obtain possession of property (e.g. from a tenant).

harbouring concealing a criminal or someone suspected of being a criminal. As an offence, it is more properly referred to as IMPEDING APPREHENSION.

harmonization the process by which member states of the European Union amend their domestic laws to make them more uniform.

hearing the trial of a case before a court, usually in public. *See also* IN CAMERA.

hearsay evidence a type of EVIDENCE that comprises statements made, or something written by, persons other than a WITNESS in court. In most cases, hearsay evidence is not admissible, but there are a number of exceptions.

heir previously, a person entitled to inherit freehold land from someone who died INTESTATE. An *heir apparent* is the person who will inherit if he outlives his ancestor; an *heir presumptive* is one whose right to inherit may be superceded by the birth of an heir with a superior claim. *See also* HEIRS OF THE BODY.

heirs of the body prior to 1925, descendants who were entitled to inherit freehold land whose owner had died INTESTATE. The laws of primogeniture apply.

High Court of Justice a court created between 1873 and 1875 and forming part of the SUPREME COURT OF JUDICATURE. It is divided into the QUEEN'S BENCH DIVISION, the CHANCERY DIVISION and the FAMILY DIVISION.

High Court of Justiciary the highest criminal court in Scotland. Appeals may be heard by the High Court sitting as the Court of Criminal Appeal. There is no right of appeal to the House of Lords.

high seas the parts of the maritime world that are not part of a territory or the internal waters of a state. *See* TERRITORIAL WATERS.

highway a road or navigable river over which the public has the right to pass. Obstructing a highway constitutes a public nuisance. *See also* FOOTPATH; OBSTRUCTION.

hijacking the unlawful seizing of an aircraft in flight by using or threatening to use force. A number of conventions have defined the offence but states are free to make their own decisions about, for example, holding hijackers and EXTRADITION.

hire (1) a contract for the temporary holding and use of another person's property, e.g. a car or piece of machinery. (2) a contract for the use of a person's services or labour in return for payment.

hire purchase a form of purchase in which the purchaser takes immediate possession of goods upon payment of a deposit and gains full ownership upon completion of a schedule of instalments over an agreed time period.

holder a person who possesses a BILL OF EXCHANGE or a promissory note. He or she may be the payee or the endorsee. A *holder in due course* is one who has taken a bill of exchange in good faith and for value before it was overdue, and without notice of any dishonour or defect in the title of the person who negotiated or transferred the bill. The holder in due course may enforce payment against all liable parties on the bill.

holding out acting in a way that leads a person to believe one has authority that does not in fact exist. By ESTOPPEL one may be prevented from denying the existence of the authority if one has represented onself as having that authority and, for example, been granted credit on the strength of it.

holding over the continued occupation by a tenant of premises after the lease has expired. The landlord may claim DAMAGES, but only if he or she does not continue to accept rent.

holograph a document written entirely in the author's handwriting.

homeless person someone who lacks accommodation. Local authorities have a legal obligation to provide accommodation for the homeless, unless they are intentionally so.

Home Office the government department responsible in England and Wales for law and order, immigration, nationality, EXTRADITION and DEPORTATION. It is headed by the Home Secretary, who has Cabinet rank.

homicide the killing of one person by another, which may be ruled lawful or unlawful. *See also* CULPABLE HOMICIDE; MANSLAUGHTER; MURDER.

honorarium a payment made as a matter of honour and not liable as a debt.

honour clause a clause in a CONTRACT that states that an agreement is only binding as a matter of honour and trust and is not legally enforceable.

hospital order an order that authorizes the holding of an offender in a specified hospital on the grounds of mental disorder.

hostage the taking of a person against his or her will and holding him or her as security against a payment or an act. *See also* HIJACKING; KIDNAPPING.

hostile witness a WITNESS who gives EVIDENCE unfavourable to the party who called him or her, but who was expected to give favourable evidence. Usually a witness cannot be cross-examined by the party calling him or her, but the judge can allow a hostile witness to be so cross-examined.

hotchpot the rule that the estate of someone who dies INTESTATE, which is to be divided equally among the beneficiaries, takes account of benefits received by any of the beneficiaries prior to the intestate person's death.

hot pursuit the pursuit in TERRITORIAL WATERS by ships belonging to a coastal state of foreign vessels believed to have contravened the pursuing state's laws. If continuous, the pursuit may extend into the HIGH SEAS but not into another state's territorial waters.

housebreaking in Scotland, an aggravated form of THEFT, which involves breaching the security of a building and entering it other than by normal means. *See also* BURGLARY.

human rights rights and protections enjoyed by people because of their humanity as opposed to rights conferred by citizenship. *See* EUROPEAN CONVENTION ON HUMAN RIGHTS.

I

ignorantia juris non excusat the doctrine that ignorance of the law is no defence against criminal or other proceedings.

illegal contract a CONTRACT that is rendered illegal because its object is criminal or immoral; because a STATUTE or common law so defines it; or because it was contracted illegally. An illegal contract is void.

illegal immigrant a person who has entered the country in contravention of immigration legislation, or who has remained in breach of a DEPORTATION order.

illegal practices *see* CORRUPT AND ILLEGAL PRACTICES.

illegitimacy being born of parents who are not married to each other. Since 1987, illegitimate children must, in almost every respect, be treated as if they were legitimate. Their parents have almost the same PARENTAL RESPONSIBILITIES as they would have were they married.

immigration entering another country with the intention of living there permanently. *See* ILLEGAL IMMIGRANT; RIGHT OF ABODE.

Immigration Appeal Tribunal a tribunal which hears appeals against decisions relating to IMMIGRATION and DEPORTATION.

immovable property things that cannot be physically moved, especially land and buildings.

immunity freedom or exemption from legal proceedings. In the UK, the sovereign enjoys immunity through the ROYAL PREROGATIVE; members of the House of Commons and the House of Lords enjoy immunity in respect of things said during a debate. *See also* DIPLOMATIC IMMUNITY.

imparlance permitting a defendant to delay answering the claim of a plaintiff to enable an attempt at amicable settlement.

impeachment the process in which the House of Commons accuses and the House of Lords judges offences against the state by persons beyond the reach of the law. In the USA, the same term is used in relation to bringing the President to justice.

impeding apprehension assisting a person known to be guilty of an offence to avoid or delay arrest and prosecution (sometimes called harbouring). Agreeing not to give information that might lead to arrest and prosecution is known as *compounding an offence*. Impeding can take other forms, such as obstructing a police officer and wasting police time by giving misleading information.

imperfect rights *see* PERFECT RIGHTS.

impersonation the offence of pretending to be another person, e.g. a police officer, juror or voter. Obtaining financial or other advantage through impersonation can constitute DECEPTION.

implied authority a type of authority implied rather than express and deriving from the terms of an agreement between principal and agent.

implied condition a condition in a CONTRACT that is implied rather than expressly written or stated. For example, in a contract of sale, it is implied that, among other things, the vendor has the right to sell the goods and that they are of MERCHANTABLE QUALITY.

implied contract a CONTRACT that exists or may be inferred from the relationship between parties or from their actions, and not expressly stated.

implied malice a state of mind that in the eyes of the law is considered sufficient for a crime, although there was not the intention of committing the crime. For example, an intention to cause GRIEVOUS BODILY HARM may be used in relation to a MURDER charge. *See also* MALICE AFORETHOUGHT.

implied term a provision in a CONTRACT that a court would consider necessary to the intentions of the parties, or which exists by STATUTE, but which was not agreed in words by the parties.

impossibility the defence that compliance with the law is physically impossible, e.g. that one cannot report an offence of which one is unaware. It is possible, however, to be convicted of attempting the impossible. *See* ATTEMPT.

impossibility of performance the impossibility of fulfilling the terms of a CONTRACT because of an event arising before or after the contract was made, which was unknown to the parties. *See also* MISTAKE OF LAW.

impotence the inability, as opposed to the refusal, of either party to a marriage to have normal sexual intercourse. If it is permanent and incurable, the marriage may be annulled. *See also* CONSUMMATION.

imprisonment committing a person convicted of an offence to a term in CUSTODY. *See* FALSE IMPRISONMENT; LIFE IMPRISONMENT; SENTENCING.

improvement notice (1) a local authority order to an owner of property to bring that property up to an accepted standard. If the owner refuses to fulfil the requirement, the authority has powers to do it at the owner's expense. (2) a requirement that a person with responsibilities for health and safety at work ensure that a breach of regulations is not repeated.

imputation an allegation made by an ACCUSED that his or her prosecutor, or any WITNESS called by the prosecutor, is of bad character or guilty of misconduct. In this event, the accused may be cross-examined about his or her own bad character or PREVIOUS CONVICTIONS.

imputation of incompetence the disparaging of a person with regard to his or her professional ability, which is actionable. *See also* DEFAMATION; SLANDER.

imputed notice the presumption the law makes that facts known to an AGENT are known to his or her PRINCIPAL, e.g. that a purchaser of land has all relevant information regarding the purchase, which is known to his or her SOLICITOR. *See also* NOTICE.

in camera literally 'in CHAMBERS', i.e. not heard in public. *See* HEARING.

incapacity a lack of the necessary legal competence to, for example, make a valid CONTRACT. In Scotland, such an incompetent person is known as *incapax*.

incest unlawful, knowing, heterosexual intercourse between members of the same family, with or without consent. The offence extends to relations between a man and his mother, daughter, sister, half-sister or grand-daughter; and between a woman and her father, son, brother, half-brother or grandfather, even in cases of ILLEGITIMACY.

inchoate not complete. Used of an action that may not itself be a complete offence but constitutes a step towards the committing of an offence, such as ATTEMPT; INCITEMENT; CONSPIRACY.

incitement the offence of persuading or attempting to persuade another person to commit an offence. If the offence is subsequently committed, the inciter may be guilty of aiding or abetting (*see* AID OR ABET). *See also* RACIAL HATRED.

incommunicado without the ability or means to communicate. Somebody detained in England should not be kept incommunicado; in Scotland, a person may be detained by the police for a fixed time without access to a SOLICITOR.

incorporeal hereditaments intangible rights over land, such as RIGHT OF WAY, right to pasture, and RIGHT OF LIGHT.

incorporeal property property which is intangible, such as COPYRIGHT, and stocks and shares.

incriminate (1) to charge with a criminal offence. (2) to suggest or indicate involvement in the committing of a criminal offence. A WITNESS may refuse to answer questions on the grounds that his or her reply might incriminate him or her. In Scotland, incrimination can be a DEFENCE, when the ACCUSED offers to show that another person committed the offence of which he or she is accused.

incumbrance *see* ENCUMBRANCE.

indecency behaviour that the average person would find shocking or revolting. *See* GROSS INDECENCY; INDECENT EXPOSURE; PUBLIC DECENCY.

indecent assault a form of ASSAULT that is considered indecent, e.g. touching a person's genitals without consent. *See* INDECENCY; GROSS INDECENCY; INDECENT EXPOSURE.

indecent exposure showing the body in a way that outrages PUBLIC DECENCY. It constitutes an offence if two people could have seen the exposure, and even if nobody was actually outraged by it. For a man to expose his genitals to a woman, in public or in private, with the intention of insulting her, is an imprisonable offence.

indemnity an agreement that one person makes to another to make good any losses suffered as a result of something owed by a third party. Unlike a GUARANTEE, indemnity is a PRIMARY RESPONSIBILITY and is not conditional on the third party being in default.

independent contractor a person or group of people employed to do work but not under contract of employment. An independent contractor is obliged to carry out the work but usually has more autonomy than an employee. A taxi driver is an independent contractor; a chauffeur is an employee.

indictable offence an offence that may be tried on INDICTMENT, i.e. by JURY in the CROWN COURT. *See also* SUMMARY OFFENCE.

indictment a document that sets out charges against a person or persons and is read to the ACCUSED at a trial. The document conforms to a standard form and lists the same details in each case. If the accused is charged with more than one offence, each is detailed in a paragraph, called a *count*.

indirect evidence *see* CIRCUMSTANTIAL EVIDENCE.

inducement the offer on the part of someone in authority (such as a police officer) to a person suspected of committing an offence of an advantage in relation to the prosecution. A CONFESSION that results from an inducement is inadmissible.

inducing breach of contract *see* PROCURING BREACH OF CONTRACT.

industrial tribunal a body authorized to hear and rule on disputes between employers and employees under the terms of employment protection legislation. Complaints include REDUNDANCY and UNFAIR DISMISSAL.

inevitable accident an accident that could not have been avoided through the exercise of normal care and skill.

infant a person below the age of 18. *See* MINOR.

infanticide the killing by its mother of a child under the age of 12 months. If the ACCUSED can show that the balance of her mind was disturbed at the time the offence was committed, she will be charged with infanticide rather than MURDER and will be sentenced as though she were guilty of MANSLAUGHTER.

in flagrante delicto *see* FLAGRANTE DELICTO.

inferior court any court that is limited in its JURISDICTION, e.g. in the type of cases it can hear. Its judgments can be appealed to a SUPERIOR COURT.

information the statement that informs a MAGISTRATE of the offence in respect of which a SUMMONS or WARRANT is requested.

informer a person who gives information to the police about criminal offences committed by other people. Although an informer enjoys no special legal status, he or she may gain an advantage if also charged with an offence, e.g. by receiving a lighter SENTENCE if convicted.

infringement the violation of the right or rights of another person.

infringement of patent *see* PATENT.

inherent vice a defect in goods which results in damage. If a carrier or insurer is not informed of an inherent vice, he or she is not liable for damage which results directly from it.

inheritance (1) the process by which property passes from a deceased person to the beneficiaries named in his or her WILL or through the provisions of the rules of INTESTACY. (2) property that a beneficiary receives from the estate of a dead person.

inheritance tax since 1986, a tax imposed on a person's INHERITANCE.

inhibition an entry in a LAND REGISTER that prohibits some specified dealing in the land for a fixed period or until a stated event occurs or a further order is made.

injunction a court order that prohibits a person from doing something (*prohibitory injunction*) or requires a person to do something (*mandatory injunction*). Often an injunction is needed urgently, when an *interlocutory injunction* is granted. A person who fails to obey an injunction is guilty of CONTEMPT OF COURT.

injurious falsehood *see* MALICIOUS FALSEHOOD.

in loco parentis literally, 'in the place of a parent'. Strictly, it applies only to people such as a GUARDIAN, who have specific responsibilities for the care of a child, but it is also commonly used of people such as FOSTER PARENTS and teachers.

Inner House *see* COURT OF SESSION.

Inner Temple one of the INNS OF COURT in the Temple in London. It is believed to have existed since the mid-15th century.

innocent misrepresentation *see* MISREPRESENTATION.

Inns of Chancery societies in which students prepared for admission to the INNS OF COURT, abolished in the late 19th century.

Inns of Court legal societies in London. Every BARRISTER must belong to one of the Inns. The four surviving are GRAY'S INN, INNER TEMPLE, LINCOLN'S INN and MIDDLE TEMPLE.

innuendo a statement by the PLAINTIFF in an action for DEFAMATION in which he or she sets out the defamatory meaning of apparently innocent words.

in personam the nature of a claim or action brought against a specific person, or a right that affects a particular person. *See also IN REM*; REAL.

inquest an inquiry into a death when the cause or causes of death are unknown, when death is sudden and unexpected, when the death is suspicious or occurs in prison, or when a CORONER has reason to believe that death was caused by violent means and cannot be attributed to natural causes. The inquest must be held before a JURY. Although an inquest is not a criminal proceeding, a WITNESS may be cross-examined by the coroner. The strict laws of EVIDENCE do not apply. An inquest may be adjourned if criminal proceedings are likely.

inquisitorial procedure a procedure that is in common use in continental Europe and consists of an inquiry into facts and circumstances and how they relate to the law. The presiding JUDGE takes an active role. *See also* ACCUSATORIAL PROCEDURE.

in re literally 'in the matter of'. These words form part of the headings of law reports along with the name of the person or subject of the case.

in rem literally 'against the thing'. The words describe a right, such as the ownership of property, as well as an action against a piece of property as opposed to a person or persons. *See also* *IN PERSONAM*.

insanity a DEFENCE based on the mental state of the ACCUSED at the time an offence was committed, such that he or she did not know what he or she was doing, or did not know that what was being done was wrong. Insanity is defined by a set of rules laid down in the middle of the 19th century, and the BURDEN OF PROOF lies with the accused as, in English and Scots law, sanity is assumed unless proved otherwise. *See* MCNAGHTEN RULES.

insanity in bar of trial a PLEA that a person cannot stand trial due to being in such a mental state as to be unable to instruct his or her DEFENCE. In such cases, a HOSPITAL ORDER may be made.

insider dealing dealing for profit in company securities on the basis of information not available to investors at large. It can be a criminal offence.

insolvency an inability to meet one's liabilities and pay debts. In Scotland, *absolute insolvency* indicates that a person's total assets would be insufficient to meet all his or her liabilities; *apparent insolvency* indicates an inability to pay debts as they fall due.

instrument a written legal document, such as a WILL OF DEED.

insufficient evidence a direction by a JUDGE to a JURY that EVIDENCE given does not entitle them to make a particular finding. If there is insufficient evidence to allow the jury to convict a person, the judge may direct it to return a verdict of NOT GUILTY.

insulting behaviour *see* THREATENING BEHAVIOUR.

insurable interest the interest a person has in the life of another person or in property such that the death of the other person or damage to, or destruction of, the property would render the first person liable or cause him or her to suffer financial loss.

insurance a CONTRACT under the terms of which the insurer agrees to make payment to the insured, in return for the payment of a premium, in the event of a particular event or against a risk.

insurance policy the INSTRUMENT that sets out the terms of a contract of INSURANCE. Such contract to be valid requires full disclosure by the insured of all facts material to the risk insured.

intangible property things owned that have no physical form, such as COPYRIGHT.

intellectual property products of the creative imagination and the intellect, such as written work, photographs, paintings, etc, that are protected by law, such as COPYRIGHT.

intention the term that describes the mental state of a person who aims to cause something to happen. Intention can itself be an offence, e.g. in the form of threatening to carry out a particular action.

intention of testator the interpretation that a court seeks to establish the intentions of a TESTATOR in his or her WILL. This need arises if a will is worded in such a way as to make its meaning unclear, where the terms appear eccentric or capricious, and if the terms of the will are challenged. *See* ARMCHAIR PRINCIPLE.

interdict in Scotland, a court order that prohibits certain behaviour. It rarely compels behaviour or action. *See also* INJUNCTION.

interest (1) a right in land and in personal property. (2) payment made by a borrower to a lender and usually paid as a percentage of the sum borrowed and within a specified time period.

interfering with trade an offence of unlawfully impeding the trade or business of another person who suffers loss as a result.

interfering with vehicles unlawfully tampering with a vehicle with the intention of stealing it or its contents, or with the intention of damaging its functions.

interfering with witnesses attempting to prevent a WITNESS from giving EVIDENCE or to influence the evidence given. *See also* CONTEMPT OF COURT; PERJURY; PERVERTING THE COURSE OF JUSTICE.

interim payment in certain circumstances, the payment on account of DAMAGES or LIABILITIES owed by the DEFENDANT to the PLAINTIFF, and made on the order of the High Court.

interim (or **interlocutory**) **relief** a temporary measure, such as an interlocutory INJUNCTION or INTERIM PAYMENT granted to the PLAINTIFF pending trial.

interlocutor in Scotland, a court order.

interlocutory appeal an APPEAL against an order made during the pre-trial (or interlocutory) stage of civil LITIGATION.

interlocutory injunction *see* INJUNCTION.

interlocutory judgment an interim judgment that deals with only parts of the case. *See also* FINAL JUDGMENT.

interlocutory proceedings the stages of civil proceedings between the originating process and the trial. They serve to define the issues that the trial will be held to decide. *See* SURPRISE.

interlocutory relief *see* INTERIM RELIEF.

internal waters the areas of water over which a state exercises JURISDICTION. They include rivers, canals, landlocked seas and lakes (except those that are in another state's territory). *See also* HIGH SEAS.

international carriage the moving of persons or goods between countries. There are a number of conventions that govern international carriage.

International Court of Justice a court of 15 judges that sits in The Hague in Holland and has powers to hear and determine disputes that relate to matters of INTERNATIONAL LAW. Each judge is elected for a period of nine years.

international law laws that address the rights and obligations of states in the ways they deal with each other. International law may also apply to the actions of multinational companies and organizations, such as the United Nations.

International Law Commission a body created under charter by the United Nations in 1947. There are 25 members, elected for five-year periods, and experts in INTERNATIONAL LAW. Its function is to develop and codify international law.

international minimum standard in INTERNATIONAL LAW, the minimum standard of treatment that a sovereign state may be expected to exercise towards nationals of other states.

interpleader summons a procedure designed to deal with conflicting claims against the same DEFENDANT.

interpretation the determining of the meaning of written documents, such as a WILL or DEED. *See* INTENTION OF TESTATOR; INTERPRETATION OF STATUTES.

Interpretation Act an Act of Parliament that standardizes the meaning of words and phrases used in other Acts with the aim of avoiding misinterpretation and misunderstanding.

interpretation clause a clause in a written document that defines words and phrases used in the document.

interpretation of statutes determining, by a set of rules and presumptions, the meaning of Acts of Parliament.

interpretation of wills the process of determining the true meaning of a WILL and the INTENTION OF TESTATOR. *See also* ARMCHAIR PRINCIPLE.

interregnum a period of time during which a throne is vacant, i.e. between the death of a sovereign and the accession of his or her successor.

interrogation the questioning, under the rules of a code of conduct, of suspects by the police. The codes confer certain rights on those being questioned. *See* CAUTION; RIGHT OF SILENCE.

interrogatory a written question put by one party to another in the course of civil LITIGATION, or to a WITNESS, that must be answered on OATH.

in terrorem literally 'by intimidation'. The term applies to, for example, a clause in a person's WILL stipulating that a gift may be withheld if the beneficiary does or does not comply with a specific condition. Such conditions are treated as 'idle threats' and are void.

interruption a break in the enjoyment of a right, which must last for at least 12 months.

intertemporal law law that is applied by international courts when a length of time has elapsed since a treaty was signed, and takes account of changes in INTERNATIONAL LAW that have occurred during the time lapse.

intestacy the situation when a person dies without having made a WILL. If there is no will, a state of *total intestacy* exists; if a will disposes of only part of the deceased's estate, it is known as *partial intestacy*. There is a set of rules governing the disposal of an intestate estate.

intimidation the use of unlawful pressure to frighten a person into doing something. Intimidation is not itself a criminal offence but may be part of a crime, e.g. intimidating a WITNESS may constitute CONTEMPT OF COURT; intimidating someone into parting with property may constitute THEFT. Intimidation is a TORT when three parties are involved, e.g. X intimidates Y into doing something to Z.

intoxication the state of being under the influence of alcohol or drugs. Drunkenness is not itself an offence but is a factor in a number of offences, including DRUNK DRIVING and being drunk and disorderly in a public place. It is an offence to supply or offer to supply to anyone under the age of 18 intoxicating liquor, or any substance, such as glue, whose fumes can be inhaled for the purposes of intoxication.

intra vires literally 'within the power'. The term describes an action carried out by a body such as a local authority that is within the powers vested in it by STATUTE. *See also* ULTRA VIRES.

inventory a list of assets or property. A tenancy agreement relating to furnished accommodation usually includes an inventory of the landlord's property that is on the premises.

invitee a person who is invited onto land or into premises for a purpose in which the occupier has a material interest, e.g. a customer in a shop. Such status is important with regard to OCCUPIER'S LIABILITY.

***in vitro* fertilization (IVF)** or **human-assisted reproduction** one of a number of techniques to achieve conception other than through sexual intercourse. These also include artificial insemination by husband or donor. Legislation has had to catch up with technological and medical progress. The legal mother is the woman who has given birth to the child; the legal father is usually the genetic father unless he is a sperm donor or the donor's sperm is used after his death. A husband may be the legal father of a child born to his wife through assisted reproduction, provided he agreed to the treatment.

involuntary conduct behaviour that cannot be controlled because of a physical or mental condition and may be used as a DEFENCE. Such defence may be unsuccessful if the sufferer acts knowing of the condition, or if the condition is self-inflicted.

irrebuttable presumption a PRESUMPTION that cannot be argued against and is effectively a mandatory rule of law.

irresistible impulse an urge to do something that the perpetrator is unable to resist. Although not usually a DEFENCE, it may be used if the impulse is attributable to certain mental conditions. *See* DIMINISHED RESPONSIBILITY; INSANITY; INVOLUNTARY CONDUCT.

irretrievable breakdown of marriage *see* BREAKDOWN OF MARRIAGE.

irrevocable authority an agency agreement that cannot be revoked. Such agreements include those that are *statutory* and designed to protect third parties against the effects of revocation of an agent's authority; and *executed authority* where the agent has already incurred liabilities as a result of his or her agency.

irrevocable letter of credit *see* LETTER OF CREDIT.

irritancy in Scotland, the termination of a LEASE following failures on the part of the TENANT, such as the non-payment of rent. A legal irritancy may be statutory.

issue (1) the matter of a court dispute. (2) descendants.

IVF *see IN VITRO* FERTILIZATION.

J

jactitation of marriage a false statement that one is married to someone. Although no longer grounds for proceedings, an injunction may be obtained to prohibit such a claim being made.

joinder of causes of action combining several causes of action against a DEFENDANT in a single action. If procedural difficulties arise, the court may order that the joinder be severed.

joinder of charges combining two or more charges of a criminal offence in a single INDICTMENT.

joinder of defendants trying two or more DEFENDANTS in the same INDICTMENT. If the defendants are indicted separately, they cannot then be tried together.

joinder of documents combining two or more documents so that together they fulfil statutory requirements.

joinder of parties two or more persons combining as DEFENDANTS or PLAINTIFFS in a single action.

joint and several a form of liability under which a person can be sued with others or individually.

joint tenancy the ownership of land or other property in which two or more persons have identical interests. If one owner dies, ownership is automatically vested in the other tenant(s), under the right of survivorship.

joint tortfeasors two or more persons responsible for a TORT, where their joint actions cause a single injury. If a single injury is caused by several people who are not acting together, they are known as *concurrent tortfeasors*.

joint venture the coming together of persons to transact a particular piece of business. Although not a continuing association, it is governed by the principles of PARTNERSHIP.

JP *see* JUSTICE OF THE PEACE.

judge an official who is empowered to adjudicate on matters brought before the courts. Judges are appointed by the Crown and are chosen from the ranks of experienced BARRISTERS and SOLICITORS. Judges may be removed from office only by a resolution that has passed through both Houses of Parliament and has received Royal Assent.

judge advocate a BARRISTER who advises on matters of MILITARY LAW that arise during the conducting of a COURT MARTIAL.

Judges' Rules prior to 1984, a set of rules governing the questioning of suspects by the police. A Code of Practice replaced Judges' Rules with the passing of the Police and Criminal Evidence Act 1984.

judgment the court's decision on a matter that has come before it. *See also* FINAL JUDGMENT; INTERLOCUTORY JUDGMENT.

judgment creditor the person named in a JUDGMENT as entitled to the benefit of the judgment.

judgment debtor the person against whom a court JUDGMENT is made and who is ordered to pay his or her debt.

judgment summons a SUMMONS for which a person entitled to enforce a JUDGMENT may apply and which requires a JUDGMENT DEBTOR to answer on OATH as to his or her means.

judicial discretion the flexibility that the court may exercise in deciding on matters such as the admission of EVIDENCE.

judicial factor in Scotland, a TRUSTEE appointed by the court to administer the estate of someone who is incapable of doing it.

judicial immunity the exemption from personal actions for DAMAGES enjoyed by a JUDGE or MAGISTRATE in the exercise of his or her office.

judicial knowledge in the law of EVIDENCE, information that the court is assumed to be aware of and so need not be proved.

judicial notice the taking by the court of certain facts as proven, when it is not necessary to hear EVIDENCE. Any facts that may be described as general knowledge (sometimes called 'notorious facts') are noticed without inquiry; others may be noticed after inquiry.

judicial precedent *see* PRECEDENT.

judicial review court control over decisions made by administrative and other official bodies, and designed to curb excessive power or the abuse of power. The court will usually only intervene if it is held that the decision is not one that any reasonable person would have made.

judicial separation a court order that states that a husband and wife do not have to live together but does not end the marriage. Such an order releases the parties from their marital responsibilities, and the court has the same JURISDICTION in matters of children and finances as in making a DIVORCE decree.

judicial trustee a TRUSTEE appointed by the court and controlled by the court.

junior barrister a BARRISTER who is not a QUEEN'S COUNSEL.

juridical relating to the law and judicial proceedings. Days on which it was permitted to conduct legal business were called 'juridical days'.

jurisdiction (1) the power of a court to hear a case and make an order. (2) the territorial area within which the court's power may be exercised.

jurisprudence (1) the study of law as a philosophy, as opposed to individual laws or legal systems. (2) the decisions of courts.

juristic person a body, such as a company, that enjoys rights and has obligations but is not a 'person' in the individual sense. *See* NATURAL PERSON.

juror a member of a JURY. Jurors are selected from the electoral roll and must meet certain criteria: age between 18 and 70; at least five years' residence in the UK since the age of 13. Several categories of persons are ineligible for jury service or may be excused, including solicitors, barristers, police officers, clergy, the mentally ill, members of Parliament, and full-time serving members of the armed forces. A DEFENDANT may challenge an individual juror who, if the challenge succeeds (i.e. it is on reasonable grounds), is replaced by another.

jury a group of JURORS (12 in England and Wales; 15 in Scotland) who are required to hear a case and reach a VERDICT. A jury is most often selected to hear criminal cases, but also a coroner's INQUEST. The jury is directed by the JUDGE on points of law and after the hearing of EVIDENCE the judge sums up for the PROSECUTION and the DEFENCE. The jury alone must then deliver a verdict, if possible unanimously. *See* GUILTY; NOT GUILTY; NOT PROVEN.

justice the protection of rights and the punishment of wrongs, which, ideally, a legal system is designed to achieve. Although the word 'justice' is widely used in the legal system, it is not synonymous with 'law'.

Justice of the Peace (JP) a person appointed by the Lord Chancellor on behalf of the Queen to carry out certain judicial duties within a specified area. Such person may sit as a MAGISTRATE and sign a WARRANT.

justification in an action for DEFAMATION, a DEFENCE that the statement made was true. Truth is a complete defence.

justify bail to show a court considering the granting of BAIL that one has the resources needed to meet the surety specified.

juvenile court a court that exercises JURISDICTION over matters relating to persons under the age of 18, including JUVENILE OFFENDERS. It is now more commonly known as a *youth court*. It is presided over by three MAGISTRATES and its proceedings are not open to the public.

juvenile offenders persons between the ages of 14 and 17 who have committed a criminal offence. Unless charged with HOMICIDE or jointly charged with another person over the age of 18, a juvenile offender will normally appear before a JUVENILE COURT. Juvenile offenders are not sentenced to prison. *See* DETENTION.

keeping the peace conduct that does not disturb public order. Courts have wide-ranging powers to require people to keep the peace. *See* BREACH OF THE PEACE.

kerb crawling the SOLICITING from a vehicle by a man of a woman for purposes of PROSTITUTION. To constitute an offence, the action must be persistent and cause annoyance to the woman in question or to other persons in the vicinity.

kidnapping taking a person away by force or fraud and against his or her will. *See also* ABDUCTION; HOSTAGE.

kleptomaniac a person suffering from a mental disorder that manifests as an irresistible urge to steal.

knock for knock a non-legal agreement between insurance companies under which an insurer will pay the loss of the person insured with it and will not raise an action against the other party's insurer. It mainly applies to motoring claims.

knock-out an illegal agreement between dealers not to bid against each other at an AUCTION.

L

label in Scotland, a piece of EVIDENCE in a criminal trial, so called because it has a label attached confirming its authenticity.

laches an unreasonable and unnecessary delay in claiming an equitable right, which denies the plaintiff the assistance of the court. The term derives from the Norman French word *lasches*, meaning 'negligence'.

land any part of the earth's surface that, in legal terms, can be owned. The term normally includes the ground below the surface and the air space above it, as well as mines and minerals, and chattels fixed to the land.

land certificate a document issued by the LAND REGISTRY giving details of the title to land and proving ownership of it. *See also* LAND REGISTRATION.

land charge a charge that binds the purchaser of land and imposes obligations in favour of another party. Examples include a mortgage that is not protected by the depositing of TITLE DEEDS, equitable EASEMENTS and RESTRICTIVE COVENANTS.

landlord a person or body who grants to another a LEASE or TENANCY, normally in return for RENT.

land registration the registering of interests in land with the LAND REGISTRY. The LAND CERTIFICATE has three parts: the *property register* describes the land; the *proprietorship register* identifies the owner; and the *charges register* lists any mortgages, covenants, etc, outstanding.

Land Registry the statutory body, established in 1862, that keeps registers of interests in land in England and Wales. It has been a government executive agency since 1990. *See* LAND REGISTRATION.

Lands Tribunal a tribunal that has jurisdiction to decide disputes arising out of the compulsory purchase of land, and disputes about the value of land or buildings, especially for the purpose of calculating inheritance tax.

lapse of gift the cancellation of a bequest because the BENEFICIARY has pre-deceased the TESTATOR. In this event, the gift becomes part of the testator's residuary estate and, subject to certain conditions, goes to the residual beneficiaries.

lapse of offer the lapsing of an offer, which may occur for several reasons, including the passage of time, the death of the recipient of the offer, and a failure to meet a particular condition. An offer to purchase goods can lapse if the goods do not remain in the same condition between offer and acceptance.

last opportunity a rule, now seldom used, that states that the last person to have an opportunity to avoid an accident is liable for it.

larceny prior to 1969, an offence that is now referred to as THEFT.

latent ambiguity *see* AMBIGUITY.

latent damage damage that is not immediately obvious. It is significant in law in terms of the length of time that has elapsed between the damage being done and a claim being brought. It is particularly important in claims for personal injury.

latent defect *see* DEFECT.

law (1) a rule that is part of a body of law. (2) the rules governing a society that may be enforced. *See* COMMON LAW; NATURAL LAW.

law agent in Scotland, a person, such as a SOLICITOR, who may practise as an agent in a court of law.

Law Commission a body established in1965 to review, develop and reform the law, to remove anomalies, repeal obsolete legislation and modernize the legal system. *See also* LAW REFORM COMMISSION.

Law Lords *see* LORDS OF APPEAL IN ORDINARY.

law merchant the practice of international merchants in commercial and maritime matters, parts of which have been absorbed into COMMON LAW.

law officers of the Crown the collective name for the ATTORNEY GENERAL, the SOLICITOR GENERAL, the LORD ADVOCATE and the SOLICITOR GENERAL FOR SCOTLAND.

Law Reform Commission a body set up by the LORD CHANCELLOR to review areas of the law that may need reform.

law reports commercial, rather than 'official', publications in which court decisions are recorded. The earliest such reports date from the 13th century.

Law Society the professional body for SOLICITORS in England and Wales. It deals with admission to practice, conduct and discipline. Solicitors may not practise unless they are issued by the Law Society with annual practising certificates.

Law Society of Scotland the professional body for SOLICITORS in Scotland. It deals with most of the same areas as its English counterpart, the LAW SOCIETY, but not discipline, which is the preserve of the Scottish Solicitors' Discipline Tribunal.

lay days (or **lying days**) the period within which cargo must be loaded onto or unloaded from a ship. The number of days is specified in a CHARTER PARTY.

laying an information making a verbal or written statement, usually by the police or a member of the public, to a MAGISTRATE, detailing an offence and the identity of the suspected offender.

leading case an important case that establishes a point of law and may be cited. *See also* PRECEDENT.

leading question a question asked of a WITNESS that itself suggests the answer or assumes the existence of disputed facts. Leading questions are not allowed except when they are formal and not disputed, and in CROSS EXAMINATION.

leapfrog a procedure for bypassing the COURT OF APPEAL and appealing direct to the House of Lords. It is rarely allowed and only when a matter of public importance in relation to the law is involved and with the consent of all parties.

lease a CONTRACT that grants the use of LAND for a specified period often in return for RENT. The contract must be in the form of a DEED that sets out the terms of the agreement. Lease also refers to the hiring of goods or equipment.

leasehold the form of ownership of property under the terms of a LEASE.

legacy a gift of PERSONAL PROPERTY under the terms of a WILL. A legacy may be *general*, e.g. a sum of money or stocks and shares, or *specific*, e.g. a particular piece of furniture or jewellery. A *demonstrative legacy* specifies a payment to be made from a named fund. A *residuary legacy* refers to all the TESTATOR's property after the repayment of any outstanding debts and the disposal of those types of legacy listed above. *See also* DEVISE.

legal aid financial assistance given to LITIGANTS whose resources are insufficient to let them use the legal process. There are stringent criteria against which an application is measured, and which take account of the type of aid applied for: assistance and advice, civil legal aid, or criminal legal aid.

legal estate the ownership of land or of an interest in land. *See* FEE SIMPLE ABSOLUTE; TERM OF YEARS ABSOLUTE.

legal fiction an assumption that extends the jurisdiction of the courts and the range of remedies. *See* LOST MODERN GRANT.

legal personality *see* PERSONALITY.

legal rights (1) all rights recognized by the law. (2) rights recognized by the common law courts and enjoyed by everyone. (3) in Scotland, the provision made by law from a person's estate for relatives of the deceased, whether or not a WILL has been made. Any estate, other than heritage, may be divided into three: for the widow or widower; for the children; and to be disposed of as willed by the deceased. *See* LEGITIM.

Legal Services Ombudsman an official appointed by the Lord Chancellor to investigate the handling by professional legal bodies of complaints. The office holder is also empowered to investigate the complaint itself.

legatee a person who is given a LEGACY.

legislation (1) the written law of a country, in the UK effectively Acts of Parliament. (2) the making of written law.

legislature the body that makes LEGISLATION; in the UK the Crown, the House of Commons and the House of Lords.

legitim in Scotland, the part of a deceased person's MOVEABLE estate that by law may be given to the child or children of the deceased: one third if the spouse survives; one half otherwise. *See* LEGAL RIGHT.

legitimacy the legal status of a person whose parents were married at the time of conception or birth.

legitimation changing a person's legal status from ILLEGITIMACY to LEGITIMACY. This can be effected by the marriage of the parents, provided the father is resident in England or Wales at the time of marriage.

lenocinium in Scotland, in family law, a wife's DEFENCE in a DIVORCE petition that her husband encouraged or connived at her ADULTERY.

lessee a person to whom a LEASE is granted. *See also* TENANT.

lessor a person who grants a LEASE to another. *See also* LANDLORD.

letter of credit a document issued by a bank undertaking and acknowledging its obligation to pay money to a third party who presents a document (such as an INSURANCE POLICY) named in the original document. An *irrevocable letter of credit* can only be revoked with the consent of the beneficiary.

letters of administration in cases of INTESTACY, authority granted to a person by the court to administer the deceased's estate. Letters of administration are also issued if the deceased person did not appoint EXECUTORS.

lewd and libidinous practice in Scotland, the crime of exposing one's genitals to young girls. *See also* INDECENT EXPOSURE.

lex causae literally 'the law of the case'. In PRIVATE INTERNATIONAL LAW, the system of law that applies to the case. *See* *LEX FORI*.

lex domicilii literally 'the law of domicile'. In PRIVATE INTERNATIONAL LAW, the law of the place where a person lives.

lex fori literally 'the law of the forum'. In PRIVATE INTERNATIONAL LAW, the law of the place where a case is heard, which governs procedure, form of TRIAL, rules of EVIDENCE, etc.

lex loci actus literally 'the law of the place where an act is carried out'. In PRIVATE INTERNATIONAL LAW, it governs matters such as the transfer of property.

lex loci celebrationis literally 'the law of the place where a marriage was celebrated'. In PRIVATE INTERNATIONAL LAW, it governs questions relating to the necessary formalities for marriage.

lex loci contractus literally 'the law of the place where a CONTRACT is made'. In PRIVATE INTERNATIONAL LAW, it governs matters relating to the making of contracts and liability.

lex loci delicti commissi literally 'the law of the place where a TORT is committed'. When accepted, in PRIVATE INTERNATIONAL LAW, it governs matters relating to liability for a tort.

lex loci situs literally 'the law of the place where something is'. In PRIVATE INTERNATIONAL LAW, it governs matters relating to ownership of and title to immoveable property.

lex loci solutionis literally 'the law of the place where a CONTRACT is performed'. In PRIVATE INTERNATIONAL LAW, it governs matters relating to the due date of payment of a BILL OF EXCHANGE.

liability (1) a legal obligation or duty. (2) an amount owed.

libel a form of DEFAMATION made in writing or in images, or in radio or television broadcasts. Unlike SLANDER, libel must be in some permanent form.

licence (1) formal permission to do something, e.g. drive a motor vehicle as a holder of a driving licence, which would otherwise be unlawful. (2) permission granted by one person to another to do something, e.g. enter land for a specified purpose.

licensed premises a place where permission has been granted for a specific activity that would otherwise be unlawful, e.g. a restaurant selling intoxicating liquor.

licensee (1) a person to whom a LICENCE has been granted for a specific activity, such as to sell intoxicating liquor. (2) a person to whom permission has been given by another person to do something, such as enter land.

lie in grant able to be transferred by DEED, e.g. land. *See also* LIE IN LIVERY.

lie in livery able to be transferred by a process of physical delivery. *See also* LIE IN GRANT.

lien a person's right to hold property belonging to another until such time as any claim against the owner has been settled. A *particular lien* confers this right only in relation to a liability against the property held; a *general lien* confers the right in relation to any or all outstanding liabilities.

life assurance *see* LIFE INSURANCE.

life estate *see* LIFE INTEREST.

life insurance or **life assurance** a form of INSURANCE, relating to the life of the insured party. *Whole-life assurance* provides for the payment of a fixed amount on the death of the insured. *Term assurance* provides for the payment of a fixed sum on the death of the insured within a specified period (e.g. 20 years). *Endowment assurance* commits the insurer to paying a fixed sum at the end of a specified period of time or on the death of the insured, if that is within the specified period.

life imprisonment a SENTENCE that commits a convicted offender to prison for the rest of his or her life. At present only MURDER carries a mandatory life sentence, although other serious crimes (such as arson) allow life as a MAXIMUM SENTENCE. In many cases, a life prisoner may in fact be released on PAROLE. *See also* MINIMUM SENTENCE.

life interest or **life estate** a person's interest in property, which lasts only for the lifetime of the grantee or the lifetime of another named party (in which case it is called 'estate *PUR AUTRE VIE*').

life tenant a person who has LIFE INTEREST in property.

lifting the veil also known as 'lifting the corporate veil', a process by which the court may look behind a company's existence as a separate legal 'person' to examine the corporation's true financial status, etc. The process is used in cases of FRAUD.

light *see* EASEMENT OF LIGHT.

limitation of actions a provision that actions cannot be brought after a statutory length of time.

limited administration authority to administer the estate of a deceased person for a limited time, e.g. if a sole EXECUTOR is a MINOR, or pending legal proceedings.

limited company a PUBLIC COMPANY that is considered to be a distinct 'person'. The members of the company have limited LIABILITY towards it.

limited executor an EXECUTOR who is appointed to deal with only part of a deceased's estate. *See also* LIMITED ADMINISTRATION.

limited liability a principle by which a shareholder in a company cannot be required to pay more than any unpaid amount in respect of his or her shares.

limited owner a person who owns an interest in property that is less than the FEE SIMPLE. *See also* LIFE TENANT.

limited partnership a combination of general partners (liable for a company's debts and obligations) and limited partners who have contributed funds or property of a stated value. *See* PARTNERSHIP

Lincoln's Inn one of the INNS OF COURT in London. Its records date from the early 15th century.

liquidated demand a demand for a specific sum of money, such as a debt, that has already been ascertained or is capable of so being. *See also* DAMAGES.

liquidation the winding-up of the affairs of a business and the conversion of assets into cash to pay off liabilities. *See also* VOLUNTARY LIQUIDATION.

liquidator a person appointed to wind up a company and bring in all the assets. Such a person must be an experienced insolvency practitioner and may call a final meeting of creditors.

lis alibi pendens literally 'suit pending elsewhere'. When LITIGATION between the same parties in relation to the same issue is pending in another JURISDICTION, a DEFENDANT may obtain a STAY OF PROCEEDINGS if he or she can show that continuing the action would be to his or her disfavour and cause an injustice.

listed building a building of special historical or architectural interest and graded according to its importance. Consent is required before such a building may be altered or demolished.

literal method a way of constructing a STATUTE so that the words in which it is expressed retain their ordinary meaning and are interpreted in the same sense as they had when the statute was passed.

litigant a party to a court action who may represent himself or herself, or be represented by a BARRISTER.

litigation (1) taking legal action. (2) the area of law concerned with contentious matters. *See* LITIGANT.

living apart as basis for DIVORCE, the recognition by a spouse that the marriage has ceased to subsist and the condition that husband and wife do not share a life together. *See also* DESERTION; SEPARATION.

living on immoral earnings living off the proceeds of PROSTITUTION. In the case of female prostitution, it is an offence with which only a man can be charged, when he knowingly lives on the earnings of a prostitute, although it is an offence for a woman to force another woman into prostitution for financial gain. In the case of male prostitution, it is an offence for a man or a woman to live off the proceeds.

living together *see* COHABITATION.

loan an arrangement where property is loaned or given by one person to another on condition that it will be returned, or where a sum of money is given on condition that it will be repaid. Various conditions usually attach to a loan, such as time, rate of interest, and, in the case of property, that it be used for the purpose agreed.

loan capital funds that are raised by a company through the issuing of debenture stock or funded debt and are repayable at a future date.

local authority a body, such as a county council, district council, parish council, etc, set up to administer the government of a specified area. Councillors are elected, usually for four years.

local government the governing in certain matters of a specified area by a LOCAL AUTHORITY.

local land charge a charge acquired by a LOCAL AUTHORITY on land, which is binding on all subsequent owners of the land; restrictions imposed by a local authority on the use of land, which binds subsequent owners of the land.

loco parentis *see* IN LOCO PARENTIS.

locus standi literally 'the right to stand'. It is the right to bring an action or to challenge a decision.

lodger a person who occupies, in return for RENT, part of a house in which the LANDLORD or his or her representative also resides.

loiter to idle in the street in a way that suggests that the loiterer has an unlawful purpose. It is an offence to loiter for the purposes of PROSTITUTION. A person may be arrested on suspicion of loitering with intent. *See* SUS LAW.

long tenancy a TENANCY that is granted for more than 21 years. The level of the RENT determines whether it is an ASSURED TENANCY or PROTECTED TENANCY.

Long Vacation the name that used to be given to the period from 1 August to 30 September when the SUPREME COURT normally only hears urgent cases (known as 'vacation business'). The rule that pleadings could not be served in the HIGH COURT during Long Vacation was abolished.

Lord Advocate the chief LAW OFFICER OF THE CROWN in Scotland and the equivalent of the ATTORNEY GENERAL in England. The Lord Advocate conducts criminal prosecutions and represents the Crown in legal proceedings in Scotland.

Lord Chancellor the head of the JUDICIARY, a member of the Cabinet, the government's legal adviser and the Speaker of the House of Lords, who presides when it sits as a COURT OF APPEAL. The Lord Chancellor appoints MAGISTRATES.

Lord Chief Justice ranking second to the LORD CHANCELLOR, the chief judge in the QUEEN'S BENCH DIVISION of the HIGH COURT. The Lord Chief Justice is appointed by the Sovereign on the Prime Minister's recommendation.

Lord Justice Clerk ranking behind the LORD JUSTICE GENERAL, the second ranking judge in Scotland, who presides over the appellate division of the COURT OF SESSION.

Lord Justice General the senior judge in Scotland, who heads the Criminal Appeal Court and is Lord President of the COURT OF SESSION.

Lords Justice of Appeal judges who sit in the COURT OF APPEAL. They are usually drawn from the ranks of HIGH COURT judges and are appointed by the Sovereign. On appointment they become members of the PRIVY COUNCIL.

Lords of Appeal in Ordinary senior judges or barristers, appointed from the COURT OF APPEAL to life peerages, who hear appeals in the House of Lords.

loss of amenity the loss or reduction of the capacity to do something as a result of personal injuries. A plaintiff in a personal injuries claim may be awarded DAMAGES for loss of amenity as well as any financial loss. It is also possible to win an award for PAIN AND SUFFERING.

lost modern grant a LEGAL FICTION that upholds a claim of EASEMENT over land belonging to another, on the assumption that it was granted by a DEED that has been lost, if the claimant can show 20 years' uninterrupted exercising of the easement.

lump sum award a once-only award of DAMAGES calculated on the financial loss incurred up to the time of trial and an estimate of future loss.

M

machinery and plant the machines and equipment purchased for the conducting of a business that qualify for a tax deduction.

magistrates voluntary officials who sit in a MAGISTRATES' COURT. They are part-time JUSTICES OF THE PEACE appointed by the Crown and usually have no formal legal training. *See also* STIPENDIARY MAGISTRATES.

magistrates' court the court where criminal prosecutions are initiated. It also has some jurisdiction over matters of debt and matrimonial proceedings. The court consists of either a number of MAGISTRATES or one STIPENDIARY MAGISTRATE.

Magna Carta the statement of a number of fundamental principles drawn up by King John and dated 15 June 1215. Among other provisions, it guaranteed the freedom of the church and promised justice for everyone in the kingdom.

main purpose rule *see* REPUGNANCY.

main residence the place where a person has lived for at least the last three years or for periods amounting to three years during the last ten. The qualification affects a claimant's rights in relation to a LEASE. In the sale of property, for capital gains tax purposes, exemption may only be claimed on the profit arising from the sale of one dwelling, which the vendor nominates as his or her main residence.

maintenance the supply of food, clothing and other necessities. Husbands are obliged to maintain their wives and vice versa, and parents their children. *See* FAILURE TO MAINTAIN. Colloquially, maintenance refers to the obligation of a spouse to support another, or a parent to support a child following DIVORCE. *See also* ALIMENT; FINANCIAL RELIEF.

maintenance agreement an agreement between spouses regarding their financial or other obligations to each other (*see also* CLEAN BREAK); a written agreement made between the father and mother of a child in respect of payments or the disposal of property to provide for the MAINTENANCE and education of the child.

maintenance order an order made against a person who has an obligation for the MAINTENANCE of another person, and providing for periodical payments.

maintenance pending suit a court order providing for periodical payments by one party to a marriage to the other party pending a DIVORCE or SEPARATION hearing, the payments to be made from the presenting of the petition to the determination of the suit.

majority the age of 18 since it was reduced from 21 in 1969, and the age at which a person is considered legally competent. *See* INFANT; MINORITY.

majority rule (1) the underlying democratic principle. (2) the principle that gives the majority of members of a company the power to control the company through voting at a meeting.

majority verdict the VERDICT of a JURY that is not unanimous. For a majority verdict to be acceptable, ten jurors must agree where there are 11 or more; nine must agree where there are ten. The jury must have had a minumum of two hours to consider its verdict; and the foreman of the jury must indicate how many members agree and disagree with the verdict.

making off without payment an offence of knowingly leaving without paying for goods or services where payment is made on the spot and with the intention of avoiding making payment.

male issue male descendants through the male line only, i.e. sons and sons and grandsons of sons, etc.

malfeasance committing an unlawful act. *See also* MISFEASANCE.

malice the attitude of a person who intentionally commits a wrong without just cause.

malice aforethought the state of mind of a person who is convicted of MURDER. There must be proved an intention to kill or to cause GRIEVOUS BODILY HARM, or an awareness that death or grievous bodily harm would almost certainly be the result of the act.

malicious arrest a form of ARREST that is made without good cause and inspired by MALICE.

malicious damage causing damage to property through unlawful and malicious acts. *See also* CRIMINAL DAMAGE.

malicious falsehood a false statement made maliciously about a person that damages his or her property or business interests. *See* SLANDER OF TITLE.

malicious mischief in Scotland, the criminal offence of damaging another person's property.

malicious prosecution proceedings shown to have been brought against a person maliciously and without reasonable cause. A person prosecuted for a criminal offence cannot claim to have been prosecuted maliciously.

malicious wounding also known as 'unlawful wounding', the offence of inflicting injury or GRIEVOUS BODILY HARM with or without using a weapon.

malingerer in a military context, a person who pretends to suffer from an illness or disability, or who inflicts self-injury to make himself or herself unfit for service.

malversation wrong behaviour by a person in a position of public trust.

mandamus literally 'we command'. An instruction by the HIGH COURT to an inferior body to carry out a specified command.

mandate an authority given by one person to another to carry out specific duties. A mandate is automatically terminated by the death of the mandator.

manslaughter unlawful killing that does not constitute MURDER and often represents a reduced charge on a number of grounds, including MITIGATION, GROSS NEGLIGENCE, and being drunk. *See also* CULPABLE HOMICIDE.

Mareva injunction the power of the court to freeze the assets held in the UK of a DEFENDANT who has left the UK and who is being sued.

marginal notes notes printed in the margins of Acts of Parliament to explain the clauses that do not constitute part of the Act.

marriage a civil or religious act or ceremony that creates the legal and social status of husband and wife and imposes obligations on both parties to one another. Nobody may marry below the age of 16. Every marriage must be registered by a marriage registrar. The parties must be of different sexes, enter the partnership willingly, and must not already be married to someone else. *See* BIGAMY.

marriage settlement an agreement made by DEED between the parties to a MARRIAGE either before or after the marriage ceremony. It relates to the settlement of property between husband and wife and can be varied by the court in the event of DIVORCE or SEPARATION.

marshalling the marshalling of funds to equalize as far as possible conflicting claims of creditors against the same debtor.

martial law government by the military when civilian rule has broken down or is unable to function for whatever reason.

Master of the Rolls a member of the HIGH COURT who presides over the civil division of the COURT OF APPEAL. The office holder's original role was as keeper of public records.

material fact (1) any fact that must be proved and is essential to a claim or defence. (2) information that, when known, must be given by a person seeking INSURANCE to the insurer.

maternity rights rights, mostly in relation to employment law, enjoyed by a woman who becomes pregnant. They include entitlement to time off work, protection of employment, maternity pay, maternity leave, etc.

matrimonial causes or **matrimonial proceedings** an action for DIVORCE, NULLITY or SEPARATION.

matrimonial home the place where a man and woman have lived together as husband and wife. The court may enforce an order giving a spouse who does not own the home certain rights of occupation. A husband has a duty to provide shelter for his wife and children; a wife must cohabit with her husband in the matrimonial home. *See* DESERTION.

matrimonial injunction a High Court or county court order restraining a party to a marriage from molesting the applicant or a child of the applicant (also called a **non-molestation order**); or excluding the party from the MATRIMONIAL HOME.

matrimonial offences conduct, such as ADULTERY, DESERTION, etc, which was the basis of a DIVORCE petition but which now only influences a court decision if extremely serious.

matrimonial order formerly, a court order for MAINTENANCE payments to be made, or affecting the custody of children.

matrimonial proceedings *see* MATRIMONIAL CAUSES.

maturity the time at which a BILL OF EXCHANGE becomes due.

McKenzie man a person who assists an unrepresented LITIGANT in court, by giving advice, making notes, etc.

McNaghten rules the rules that govern whether or not a plea of INSANITY is accepted in mitigation of an indictable offence.

maximum sentence, fine, etc the harshest punishment prescribed by the law for a specific offence.

measure of damages the principle upon which DAMAGES are calculated when a plaintiff has successfully brought an action for TORT or BREACH OF CONTRACT.

mediation the intervention of a third party to resolve a dispute between two other parties.

memorandum in writing previously, a document in writing and signed by the parties which was evidence of a contract for the sale of land. Now all such contracts must be in writing.

memorandum of association a document that must be drawn up when a REGISTERED COMPANY is formed. It must be signed by two or more founder members, and gives the company's name and address and the nature of its business.

mens rea literally 'guilty mind'. The prosecution must prove that an accused person was of this state of mind in order to secure a conviction. It varies from crime to crime, but generally the accused must have intended to do wrong, or at least knew that he or she was doing wrong.

mercantile agent an AGENT authorized to buy or sell goods or to raise money on the security of goods on behalf of a PRINCIPAL.

merchantable quality the condition of goods that are fit for the purpose for which they are sold and that match any description made of them within reasonable limits.

mercy the Crown's prerogative to commute or suspend a SENTENCE. It is known as the **prerogative of mercy**.

mercy killing the offence of unlawfully killing another person believed to be suffering and whose condition is incurable. It is also referred to as **euthanasia**.

merger (1) the joining together of two commercial companies of roughly equal size. The members of both companies exchange their shares for shares in the new merged company. (2) the vesting in one person of two estates or interests in land, usually by absorbing a lesser interest into a greater one.

mesne profits a LANDLORD's claim for payment from a tenant who continues to occupy property after the end of the TENANCY. The landlord may claim an amount that matches the current market rent for the property.

messuage a dwelling house together with adjoining buildings, garden and orchard.

Metropolitan stipendiary magistrate a full-time paid MAGISTRATE who sits in the Metropolitan Stipendiary Courts. *See* STIPENDIARY MAGISTRATES.

Middle Temple one of the four INNS OF COURT in London. Its earliest records date from the early 15th century. Its premises between the Strand and the Embankment were granted in perpetuity in 1609.

military courts *see* COURT MARTIAL; COURT OF CHIVALRY.

military law *see* SERVICE LAW.

minumum sentence, fine, etc the most lenient punishment that the law prescribes may be imposed for a specific offence.

mining lease a LEASE of up to 100 years granted to a TENANT FOR LIFE for the extraction of minerals from the land, usually in return for a RENT.

ministerial responsibility the responsibility to Parliament of Ministers of the Crown, individually and collectively, for actions of their departments, whether or not personally authorized.

Minister of the Crown the holder of an office in the UK Government, appointed by the Crown on the advice of the Prime Minister of the day.

minor a person below the age of 18. *See also* INFANT; MAJORITY.

minor interests in LAND REGISTRATION, interests that cannot be created or transferred by registered dispositions and that can be overridden by a proprietor. *See* OVERRIDING INTERESTS.

minority (1) being below 18 years of age (*see* MAJORITY). (2) the smaller group at an assembly or in a voting procedure.

minority protection rules that safeguard minority shareholders from abuse by majority shareholders in a company. Remedies include just and equitable WINDING UP, and seeking an investigation of the company.

minutes the record of a meeting kept in the form of notes. Registered companies are required by law to keep minutes of general meetings, board meetings, etc.

misadventure a cause of death that is not the result of criminal action or negligence. A CORONER may deliver a VERDICT of death by accident or misadventure, which are not distinguished.

misappropriation the dishonest taking of another's property.

miscarriage of justice a failure in the administration of JUSTICE, for which compensation may be paid.

mischief a term found in the 'mischief of a STATUTE', being the wrong for which the statute is intended to provide the remedy.

misdemeanour the old name for an offence that was not serious enough to be called a FELONY. The distinction between misdemeanours and felonies was abolished in 1967.

misdescription a false or misleading description of the subject matter of a CONTRACT, usually of property for sale. A purchaser may sue for DAMAGES if loss is incurred as the result of a misdescription of property in the contract of sale.

misdirection the failure of a JUDGE properly and correctly to direct a JURY on EVIDENCE and points of law. Misdirection can be grounds for an APPEAL and, if successful, a conviction can be quashed.

misfeasance the improper performance of an otherwise lawful act. *See* MALFEASANCE.

misjoinder of parties the wrongful JOINDER OF PARTIES in an action, which can be remedied by an AMENDMENT.

misnomer giving a person a wrong name in PLEADINGS.

mispleading the omission in PLEADINGS of some essential part of an allegation, rectifiable by AMENDMENT.

misprision the failure to report an offence. The crime of 'misprision of felony' has been replaced by *compounding an offence* (*see* IMPEDING APPREHENSION) but may still be brought in the case of TREASON.

misrepresentation the misrepresentation of a material fact with the intention of inducing another person into entering into a CONTRACT. *Fraudulent misrepresentation* is made knowing it to be false, or with reckless disregard for its truth or falseness. *Innocent misrepresentation* implies there is no fault. *Negligent misrepresentation* is a statement made by a person who has no reasonable grounds for believing it to be true.

mistake of law an error about a matter of law, which nevertheless does not affect the validity of an agreement. It may be in the form of a misunderstanding or an erroneous belief.

mistrial a TRIAL that is defective and therefore false.

mitigation the lessening or 'softening' of a penalty. A plea made in mitigation of SENTENCE is not based on any material fact that might have formed part of the DEFENCE but on personal circumstances, family responsibilities, damage to career prospects, etc. A reduction in DAMAGES as a result of TORT or BREACH OF CONTRACT; the plaintiff is required, as far as is reasonably possible, to minimize the loss he or she suffers.

mixed action a court action in which a claim relating to property is combined with a claim for DAMAGES.

mixed fund a fund made up from the proceeds of the sale of both real and personal property.

mixed property something owned and made up of a combination of real and personal property. *See* EMBLEMENT.

mock auction an offence covering the sale by AUCTION of a range of goods where articles are given away, the right to bid is restricted to persons who have agreed to buy an article, a lot is sold to a bidder at a price below his or her highest bid for it, or part of the price bid is repaid or credited to the bidder.

molestation conduct that annoys or injures, or is intended to annoy or injure other persons, usually one's spouse and children. Such conduct includes persistently following, harassment and making threatening telephone calls.

money Bill a bill introduced in Parliament that relates only to matters of taxation. It is for the Speaker's judgment whether or not a bill may be so designated.

money had and received formerly, the possession by the DEFENDANT of money that rightfully belongs to the PLAINTIFF, as, for example, when an AGENT is in receipt of money destined for his or her PRINCIPAL but fails to pass it on.

money laundering the colloquial term for passing the proceeds of crime through the financial system in order to conceal their origins. It is an offence to fail to report suspicions of money laundering, a provision that has placed considerable responsibility on institutions such as banks and building societies.

moneylender a person who makes a business of lending money. The original Acts regulating moneylenders did not cover such bodies as banks, insurance companies and building societies, nor pawnbrokers. Regulation is now governed by the Consumer Credit Act 1974.

Monopolies and Mergers Commission a body appointed by the Secretary of State to investigate the existence or possible existence of a MONOPOLY, which may arise following a MERGER.

monopoly a market in which a sole supplier operates and in which there is consequently no competition.

moratorium a period when an authorized delay in meeting an obligation, e.g. the repayment of a debt, is in force.

mortgage security for a loan in the form of an interest in property. The interest is terminated when the debt is repaid. Although the *mortgagee* (the lender) may take possession of the property as soon as the mortgage is made, that right is subject to a number of restrictions. The borrower is known as the *mortgagor*. The most common form of mortgage relates to the purchase of buildings and land. *See* MORTGAGE ACTION.

mortgage action court action taken by the mortgagee (the lender) to possess the mortgaged property (commonly known as 'repossession') or to recover the whole debt, when the mortgagor (the borrower) has failed to make the agreed repayments.

motion (1) a formal proposal made at a meeting. (2) an oral application made to a JUDGE in open court requesting an order requiring an action favourable to the applicant.

motive the reason for which somebody does something. In legal actions, motive is not usually relevant in deciding guilt or innocence but may influence the level of punishment on conviction. *See also* MENS REA.

moveables personal property, as opposed to 'real' property such as land and buildings.

mugging a colloquial term for ROBBERY from a single pedestrian.

multiple admissibility in the rules of EVIDENCE, the principle that evidence admissible for one purpose may not be rejected solely because it is inadmissible for another purpose.

multiple damages an amount of DAMAGES, calculated by multiplying the sum that would be compensatory. This entitles a UK resident to claim against an award made in another country.

multiple poinding in Scotland, a procedure that combines the pleas of all parties claiming an interest in a fund, allowing them to be heard in a single action.

municipal law the law of one nation or state, as opposed to the law of nations, or INTERNATIONAL LAW.

muniments documents, including TITLE DEEDS, that prove a person's title to land.

munitions arms, ammunition, explosives, etc, and anything that is used in their manufacture.

murder unlawful homicide with MALICE AFORETHOUGHT. To secure a conviction, the prosecution must show that the accused intended to kill or cause serious harm to the victim. The Crown must prove *MENS REA*, i.e. intention or wicked disregard for the consequences. *See also* ATTEMPTED MURDER; MANSLAUGHTER.

mute *see* STAND MUTE.

mutiny an offence against SERVICE LAW in which a member of the armed forces combines with one or more other persons to overthrow or resist lawful authority, to disobey such authority or to impede the performance of any duty.

mutual wills an arrangement in which two or more persons draw up a WILL conferring reciprocal benefits, i.e. in favour of each other. Such wills may be revoked during the lifetime of all TESTATORS, but a court will enforce the terms of the mutual wills following the death of any of the testators.

N

naked agreement a non-binding agreement that has been made without the benefit of CONSIDERATION, i.e. a promise by one party to a CONTRACT constituting the price for which he or she buys the promise of the other party.

naked trust or **bare trust** a TRUST that does not require a TRUSTEE to perform any duties but merely to hold the property in trust and to hand over the property to the person entitled to it at that person's request.

name, change of *see* DEED POLL.

name and arms clause a clause in a WILL that specifies that a beneficiary may only benefit if he or she uses a precisely specified surname and, if appropriate, coat of arms.

national conditions of sale a set of standard conditions used by SOLICITORS in drawing up closed contracts for the sale of land. *See* OPEN CONTRACT.

nationality the legal relationship between an individual and a state that results from birth, marriage or NATURALIZATION. In most cases, citizenship confers rights and protections, and imposes obligations and allegiances.

natural child an illegitimate child. *See* ILLEGITIMACY.

naturalization a process by which a person becomes a BRITISH CITIZEN. It is granted by the Secretary of State to persons who have satisfied the required conditions, including five years' residence (three years for the spouse of a British citizen), proficiency in one of the languages of the British Isles, and the swearing of an OATH OF ALLEGIANCE.

natural justice the principle that the decision of a court be without bias, i.e. made by an impartial judge with no personal interest in the outcome, and that the person directly affected by the decision is given an opportunity to state his or her case and to know and answer the other side's case.

natural law the basis of law developed by the ancient Greeks and an important part of JURISPRUDENCE. It is based on the idea that nature confers on humankind a form of perfect justice that human laws should match as far as possible. *See also* POSITIVE LAW.

natural person a human being in the normal sense of the term. A company may be described as an artificial or 'legal' person. *See* JURISTIC PERSON.

natural rights rights conferred on people by the NATURAL LAW. An acceptance of the existence of such rights has influenced, for example, the legal history of the USA.

naval court a court made up of merchant naval officers and summoned by the commander of a naval vessel on foreign station to investigate the loss of a ship or a complaint made by an officer or seaman.

naval law *see* SERVICE LAW.

navigation rights the public's entitlement to use a river or other inland water as a HIGHWAY.

necessaries the goods and services required by a MINOR or by a person suffering from some incapacity. These include essential clothing. A reasonable price must be paid for necessaries sold to such a person.

necessity circumstances that make a course of action unavoidable and that compel one to commit an illegal act. As a DEFENCE, its success is unpredictable. It may succeed if it can be shown that the damage done by an act is the result of an attempt to avoid greater damage. It would not, though, be a defence to charges of MURDER or THEFT.

negative pregnant a literal but evasive answer to a question in PLEADINGS. If X denies receiving £10,000 from Y but in fact received a smaller sum, the answer is a negative pregnant if the issue underlying the question was the receipt by Y of any amount of money at all. *See also* AFFIRMATIVE PREGNANT.

negative prescription *see* PRESCRIPTION.

neglect the culpable failure to carry out a duty. It is a criminal offence for a parent to neglect his or her child knowing that the child will be caused suffering or injury as a result. *See also* NEGLIGENCE.

negligence the breach of a duty that results in damage to the person to whom the duty was owed. The standard against which professional negligence is measured is the skill of the average member of the profession. Negligence may be an element in the committing of a serious crime, such as MANSLAUGHTER. Negligence may the breach of a duty of care; *see* NEGLECT. *See also* CONTRIBUTORY NEGLIGENCE; CRIMINAL NEGLIGENCE; GROSS NEGLIGENCE.

negligent misrepresentation *see* MISREPRESENTATION.

negotiable instrument a document that constitutes an obligation to pay a sum of money, which is payable by delivery so that the present holder can sue in his or her own name. If on transfer the document is accepted in good faith, the transferee can enforce the obligation even if the transferor's title is defective. Negotiable instruments include dividend warrants, promissory notes and BILLS OF EXCHANGE.

negotiation of a bill the transfer of a BILL OF EXCHANGE from one person to another. The transferee becomes the holder of the bill.

nemo dat quod non habet literally 'no one can give that which he has not'. The principle that a person cannot, without the authority of the true owner, confer property that he or she does not own, such as stolen property. However, there are exceptions, including sales made under a court order.

nemo debet bis vexari literally 'no man ought to be twice vexed'. The principle that no person should be prosecuted twice for the same offence provided a competent court has made a final decision.

nemo debet esse judex in propria causa literally 'no person should be a judge in his own cause'. The rule also applies to any cause in which the person has an interest.

nemo est heres viventis literally 'no one is the heir of a living person'. A person's heir cannot be ascertained until that person's death. An HEIR APPARENT, therefore, has no legal interest in property that he or she expects to inherit until it actually devolves upon him or her.

nemo tenetur seipsum accusare literally 'no person is bound to incriminate himself'.

neonate a newborn child.

nervous shock recognized physical or psychiatric illness caused by shock. Persons involved in an accident can recover DAMAGES for suffering shock.

net estate the property that a deceased person can dispose of by WILL, less funeral, testamentary and administrative expenses.

next friend an adult through whom legal proceedings are conducted on behalf of an INFANT or a mentally incapacitated person.

next of kin one's closest blood relations. The relationship between parents and children is considered to be the closest.

nisi literally 'not final'. *See* DECREE NISI.

no case to answer a defendant's submission, at the end of a plaintiff's or the prosecution case, that he or she need not make reply because there are insufficient legal grounds, or insufficent evidence has been presented, in other words, that there is no case to answer.

no-fault the principle that a person should be able to receive compensation for injury without having to prove that anyone else is at fault.

nolens volens literally 'whether willingly or unwillingly'.

nolle prosequi literally 'unwilling to prosecute', a plaintiff's undertaking not to continue an action. The ATTORNEY GENERAL may halt criminal proceedings when, for example, the ACCUSED cannot be brought to court to stand trial because of long-term physical or mental incapacity. It does not constitute an ACQUITTAL, and proceedings may be brought at a later date.

nolo contendere literally 'I do not wish to contend', which usually implies a confession of GUILT.

nominal damages an amount of DAMAGES awarded when no substantial loss has been suffered but when the plaintiff's legal rights have been infringed. It has been known for a successful plaintiff to be awarded damages of one penny.

nomination a direction to a person holding funds that they should be paid to a named person on the death of the person issuing the direction. This may be done by anyone of age 16 or over.

nonage the time when a person is below the age of 18. *See* MAJORITY.

non-cohabitation order a magistrate's order freeing a wife from the obligation of living with her husband. Such orders were abolished in 1978, but those in force before that date may still have force. A woman awarded such an order cannot be guily of DESERTION.

non compos mentis literally 'not of sound mind'.

non constat literally 'it is not clear' or 'it does not follow'.

non-contentious business business, usually conducted by a SOLICITOR, that is not involved with LITIGATION, e.g. drawing up a WILL.

non-delivery a BREACH OF CONTRACT through a failure to deliver goods, which may give grounds for an action for DAMAGES.

non-direction the failure of a JUDGE to give direction to the JURY on a point of law. *See also* MISDIRECTION.

non-disclosure, also known as **concealment**, failure to make known relevant information, especially in the process of drawing up a CONTRACT, which would influence the other party's decision as to whether or not to enter into the contract. It also applies in cases where a person seeking INSURANCE cover fails to give all relevant, material information to the insurer.

non-discrimination notice a notice requiring a person or persons not to commit acts of RACIAL DISCRIMINATION or SEX DISCRIMINATION.

non est factum literally 'it is not his deed'. A plea that a document is not that of the DEFENDANT, used in cases where there has been a MISTAKE OF LAW in the transaction and the defendant was unaware of the true nature of it.

nonfeasance failure to perform an act that one is lawfully bound to do. It has been ruled that the distinction between nonfeasance and MALFEASANCE is valid only in the case of HIGHWAY repair and any action brought as a result of injuries caused by a failure to keep highways in good repair.

non-joinder a plea in ABATEMENT that a plaintiff has failed to join an action to which he or she should have been a party. *See* JOINDER OF PARTIES.

non-jury list a list of cases to be heard in the QUEEN'S BENCH DIVISION by a judge sitting alone or with ASSESSORS.

non-molestation order *see* MATRIMONIAL INJUNCTION; MOLESTATION.

non-provable debt a type of debt that cannot be claimed in the event of BANKRUPTCY.

non-suit (1) the renouncing of a suit by the PLAINTIFF before a VERDICT because of a defect in the case. (2) the withdrawal by a JUDGE from a JURY of a suit and the direction of a verdict in favour of the ACCUSED.

non-user failure to exercise a right over land. If non-use continues for a sufficient length of time, the right may be extinguished.

notary or **notary public** a legal official, usually a SOLICITOR, who attests DEEDS and protests dishonoured bills. *See* PROTEST.

not guilty (1) a plea that constitutes a challenge to the PROSECUTION to prove guilt. (2) following a trial, a VERDICT that is an ACQUITTAL. *See also* GUILTY.

notice knowledge of a fact. *Actual notice* is knowledge held; *constructive notice* is knowledge that a person could reasonably be expected to hold; *imputed notice* is actual or constructive knowledge held by one acting as one's AGENT. Notice also refers to notification, given by an employer or employee, of the termination of a contract of employment.

notice of abandonment *see* ABANDONMENT.

notice of discontinuance notice served by a PLAINTIFF or a DEFENDANT that voluntarily terminates an action. If served within less than 14 days, the consent of the court or of all parties to the action is required.

notice of dishonour notice given by the holder of a BILL OF EXCHANGE to any parties held liable that it has been dishonoured.

notice of intended prosecution notice served in writing on a person charged with certain motoring offences that he or she will be prosecuted.

notice of title knowledge (*see* NOTICE) held by an intending purchaser of land that title is encumbered by rights or interests, i.e. that other parties enjoy rights or interests.

notice to produce notice given by one party in an action to another to produce documents that he or she holds. Failure to produce said documents at trial may result in SECONDARY EVIDENCE of documents being given.

notice to quit formal notification given by a LANDLORD or TENANT of the termination of a tenancy agreement. The form of the notice is subject to a number of statutory requirements.

noting a bill the attachment by a NOTARY of a memorandum to a BILL OF EXCHANGE, giving the reason for which it has been dishonoured. *See* PROTEST.

not negotiable words written or printed on a cheque, postal order, etc, indicating that the holder enjoys no better right to it than the previous holder.

notorious facts matters of common knowledge of which judicial notice may be taken.

not proven in Scotland, a VERDICT that reflects the insufficiency of the prosecution case yet acknowledges doubt about the innocence of the accused. For practical purposes it amounts to a NOT GUILTY verdict; the accused is released and may not be tried for the same offence again.

novation the replacing of an existing CONTRACT with a new one between the same parties or introducing a new party. It is used to substitute one debtor for another.

novus actus interveniens literally 'a new act intervening' or ***nova causa interveniens***, 'a new cause intervening'. An event, such as an act by a third party, that intervenes between an act or omission and the damage done by it, and that can relieve the defendant of responsibility for the damage caused.

noxious offensive, tending to damage health, as in noxious fumes.

nudum pactum literally 'NAKED AGREEMENT', i.e. one without CONSIDERATION.

nugatory useless, invalid.
nuisance interference with a person's enjoyment of, or right to, land is PRIVATE NUISANCE (a TORT); interference with the health or safety of other people in general is PUBLIC NUISANCE (a CRIME).
null and void invalid, without force.
nulla poena sine lege literally 'no punishment without a law'. A person may only be punished for a crime if the punishment is prescribed by statute. The punishment may be mandatory (as life imprisonment for murder or treason, *see* MANDATE) or a MAXIMUM or MINIMUM sentence, fine, etc.
nullity of marriage invalidity of a marriage due to a number of causes. The marriage may be void if, at the time of marriage, either party was under the age of 16, the parties fall within PROHIBITED DEGREES OF RELATIONSHIP, or either party was already lawfully married; the marriage may be voidable if, at the time of marriage, there was a lack of valid consent, the female partner was pregnant by a man other than her husband, or there is an unwillingness or inability to consummate the marriage.
nullum crimen sine lege literally 'no crime without a law'. Also known as the *principle of legality*, the principle that conduct is only a CRIME if the law has declared it to be so.
nunc pro tunc literally 'now for then', describing a judgment that has effect from an earlier date than that on which it is given.
nuncupative will an oral (rather than written) TESTAMENT directing how property is to be disposed of after death. It is ineffective except as a PRIVILEGED WILL.

O

oath a sworn appeal (usually to God) that a statement is true or that a promise is binding. An oath is required in the case of an AFFIDAVIT or when giving EVIDENCE. If a person objects to invoking the name of God, he or she may AFFIRM instead. *See also* COMMISSIONER FOR OATHS.

oath of allegiance (1) an oath sworn by officers of the Crown on their appointment. (2) an oath sworn by persons in the process of NATURALIZATION.

obedience to orders a defence that one was acting on the orders of a superior and *MENS REA* cannot be shown.

obiter dictum literally 'a remark in passing', a statement by a judge when giving judgment based on facts that were not presented or were not material to a case. *See also* PERSUASIVE AUTHORITY.

objection (1) in court proceedings, an intervention by COUNSEL that asserts that a question put by opposing counsel is improper and should be disallowed, or that a document or exhibit should not be received. (2) in planning law, opposition to an application to build, alter, etc, a building, which plans have had to be advertised so that objections can be raised. *See also* OBJECTION TO INDICTMENT.

objection to indictment a procedure whereby an ACCUSED attempts to show that the INDICTMENT is open to legal objection, e.g. because it fails to comply with an enactment.

obligation (1) a legal or moral duty to take a course of action. (2) a BOND with a condition attached, such as a penalty for failure to fulfil.

obligee a person to whom one (the obligor) is bound by a BOND.

obligor a person who is bound to another (the obligee) by a BOND.

obliteration an alteration to a WILL made by rendering words indecipherable. The alteration is valid if the obliterated words cannot be read or it is signed and witnessed.

obscene publications printed material, or televised screenings and theatre performances, which 'tends to deprave and corrupt' any person who sees or reads it. It is an offence to publish, offer for sale, distribute, lend, hire or send by post any obscene article. A JURY must decide in fact whether or not an article is obscene; the MOTIVE of the writer, publisher, etc, is irrelevant.

obscene telephone call the summary offence of making a telephone call that would 'tend to deprave and corrupt' the person receiving the call. *See also* OBSCENE PUBLICATIONS.

obstructing a police officer hindering, by physical force, threats, lying, giving misleading information or helping an offender to escape detection, of a police officer in the performance of his or her duty.

obstructing the highway the offence of removing part or all of the HIGHWAY from use by the public.

obstruction the offence of impeding other road users with a vehicle, such as by blocking a thoroughfare or driving unreasonably slowly.

obstruction of recovery of premises the offence of resisting or preventing a lawful possession process by court officers against unauthorized occupiers of land or buildings.

occupancy taking possession of property, such as land, that has no owner.

occupant (1) a person who resides in a place. (2) a person who acquires land or buildings by OCCUPANCY.

occupier a person who possesses land or buildings, as owner or tenant. A TRESPASSER may become an occupier if the landowner accepts RENT from him or her.

occupier's liability (1) the liability that the person occupying land or buildings has with regard to anyone on the premises. (2) the DUTY OF CARE that he or she has.

occupying tenant a person who occupies a dwelling as a TENANT or LESSEE, and not as the OWNER-OCCUPIER.

offence the term usually employed to refer to a CRIME. *See* ARRESTABLE OFFENCE; INDICTABLE OFFENCE; SUMMARY OFFENCE.

offences against international law acts or omissions that are in breach of INTERNATIONAL LAW, such as HIJACKING and PIRACY.

offences against property acts or omissions that affect a person's rights of ownership, such as ARSON; BURGLARY; CRIMINAL DAMAGE; DECEPTION; FORGERY; MAKING OFF WITHOUT PAYMENT.

offences against public order acts or omissions that impede the functioning of an ordered society, such as AFFRAY; OBSTRUCTION; RIOT; THREATENING BEHAVIOUR.

offences against the person acts or omissions that involve the use or threat of physical violence against another person, such as ASSAULT; GRIEVOUS BODILY HARM; HOMICIDE; KIDNAPPING; RAPE.

offences against the state acts or omissions that threaten the security of the state, such as SEDITION; TERRORISM; TREASON.

offences relating to road traffic acts or omissions relating to driving on public roads, such as CARELESS AND INCONSIDERATE DRIVING; DANGEROUS DRIVING; DRUNK DRIVING; SPEEDING.

offence triable either way a crime that may be tried as an INDICTABLE OFFENCE or a SUMMARY OFFENCE. The category includes BIGAMY; DECEPTION; THEFT.

offender a person who is guilty of committing a CRIME. *See* FIRST OFFENDER; FUGITIVE OFFENDER; PERSISTENT OFFENDER.

offensive weapon any article that has been made or adapted, or is intended, to cause physical injury. It is an offence to have, without authority or reasonable cause, such an article in a public place. A household utensil, such as a carving knife, may be classified as an offensive weapon if it is wielded in public.

offer a written or oral proposal to enter into a legally binding CONTRACT. It may be express or implied.

offer for sale a document issued by a body that has purchased shares in a public company, offering the shares to the public.

Official Custodian for Charities a person who acts in the role of a TRUSTEE for charitable bodies and in whom charity property is vested by court order.

official receiver a person appointed by the Secretary of State for Trade and Industry in matters concerning BANKRUPTCY. The functions include managing the estate of a debtor and convening a first meeting of creditors.

official referee prior to 1972, a judge appointed to consider matters such as arbitration agreements and lengthy and complex trials involving substantial technical detail.

official search an enquiry into land registers to ascertain the existence of encumbrances on land. The search is made on an application by an intending purchaser who seeks an official certificate relieving him or her of liability regarding any rights that the official search has not discovered.

official secrets matters relating to the security of the state and defined by a number of Official Secrets Acts. It is an offence to enter a prohibited place or to use certain types of information in such a way that is prejudicial to state security. It is also an offence to receive such information.

Official Solicitor an official who acts as NEXT FRIEND in court proceedings for anyone who is unrepresented and unable to represent himself or herself. The holder may also be required to intervene to protect the interests of children in certain actions.

Old Bailey *see* CENTRAL CRIMINAL COURT.

ombudsman *see* LEGAL SERVICES OMBUDSMAN.

omission (1) a failure to act in circumstances when one has a duty to act (*see* DUTY OF CARE; NEGLIGENCE; OCCUPIER'S LIABILITY). (2) a blank space in a document.

omnia praesumuntur contra spoliatorem literally 'all things are presumed against a wrongdoer'. *See* PRESUMPTION.

onerous burdensome. In a case of BANKRUPTCY, a TRUSTEE may disclaim onerous property, such as unsaleable goods or worthless contracts.

onus probandi *see* BURDEN OF PROOF.

open contract a CONTRACT for the sale of land, which details only the names of the parties, the property and the price to be paid. *See* FORMAL CONTRACT.

open court a court that offers access to the public. *See* *IN CAMERA*.

opening speech (1) the speech made by prosecuting counsel at the beginning of a criminal trial, outlining the allegations against the defendant and the evidence to be introduced. (2) at the beginning of a civil trial, the speech made by defence counsel.

open justice the doctrine underlying the assertion that 'justice should not only be done but should manifestly and undoubtedly be seen to be done'.

open space land of which not more than a twentieth part is covered with buildings or on which there are no buildings. The land may or may not be enclosed. It is often in an area designated a 'conservation area' by the Secretary of State for the Environment.

open verdict a VERDICT in a CORONER's court that leaves open the question of how a person met his or her death. *See* INQUEST.

operative part the part of a DEED that effects the principal object of the deed. *See also* RECITALS.

operative words the exact words in a document that effect the purpose of the document. As long as the intention is unambiguous, no particular form of words is required.

opinion (1) a judgment delivered by the House of Lords. (2) when applied to COUNSEL, the advice of a BARRISTER on a specific question. *See also* EXPERT WITNESS.

opinions in evidence the beliefs or opinions of non-expert persons (*see* EXPERT WITNESS) offered as EVIDENCE. As evidence is usually concerned with provable facts, opinions are not usually admissible, although there are a few exceptions, such as a belief about how fast a car was travelling or questions of identity.

oppression (1) a disregard of the essentials of justice. (2) a vindictive punishment out of proportion to the severity of the crime.

option the right to accept or reject an OFFER, usually within a specified time. For an OPTION TO PURCHASE to be valid, the price must be stated or a means specified of fixing the price at a subsequent date.

option to purchase the right to compel the owner of land to sell it to the holder of the option on the terms agreed.

oral agreement a CONTRACT made by word of mouth, rather than in writing. *See* IMPLIED CONTRACT.

oral evidence EVIDENCE given in court by word of mouth, usually on OATH. It consists of what the WITNESS perceived through his or her senses; it may also be HEARSAY EVIDENCE.

orality examination of witnesses whose evidence must be given orally unless on AFFIDAVIT.

oral will *see* NUNCUPATIVE WILL.

orders (1) court directions. (2) a division of the rules of the SUPREME COURT.

Orders in Council legislative orders made by the Sovereign and the PRIVY COUNCIL, or by the government sanctioned by the Privy Council. Such Orders can be used to bring Acts of Parliament into force.

Orders of Council legislative orders made by the PRIVY COUNCIL alone. *See* DELEGATED LEGISLATION.

ordinance (1) legislation under the ROYAL PREROGATIVE. (2) a Parliamentary decree that does not have the consent of the House of Lords.

ordinarily resident a term used to describe a person who lives in a particular place voluntarily or for a particular purpose.

ordinary resolution a decision made by a simple majority of the members of a company, voting in person or by PROXY. *See also* SPECIAL RESOLUTION.

ordinary share a SHARE in a company, carrying the greatest risk and ranking for repayment of capital and the payment of dividends behind debenture and preference shares.

original evidence indirect evidence of a statement made other than by the testifying WITNESS. The evidence offered is that the statement was made, rather than the truth of the statement. *See* DIRECT EVIDENCE.

originating summons a HIGH COURT process in cases involving questions of law and the interpretation of documents. The summons includes the questions on which the PLAINTIFF will be seeking direction or a decision by the court. *See also* WRIT.

ostensible authority a type of authority that is suggested by circumstances and appearances but may not be the same as actual authority.

ouster an act, such as ADVERSE POSSESSION, that wrongfully deprives a person of freehold title or other inheritance.

ouster clause a clause in a STATUTE that excludes judicial proceedings in matters of dispute. The norm is that documents, contracts, etc, do not exclude the jurisdiction of the courts.

ouster order a court order that prohibits or suspends a spouse's right to occupy the MATRIMONIAL HOME.

outer Bar or **utter Bar** a term used to describe JUNIOR BARRISTERS who plead 'outside the bar'.

outstanding offences offences that may be taken into consideration by the court when determining sentence. They must be similar to the offence of which the defendant is convicted and must be within the jurisdiction of the court.

outstanding term a period of time that has not ended when the purpose for which it was created has been fulfilled. *See also* SATISFIED TERM.

overcrowding the occupation of a dwelling by a number of people, which contravenes statute. The overcrowding may relate simply to numbers or to the number of dwellers relative to the number of rooms, floors, etc.

overdue bill a BILL OF EXCHANGE that is in circulation for an unreasonably long time after payment was due.

overriding interests rights and interests in land, which bind the proprietor and a third party who acquires the land or an interest in it but which cannot be protected by registration.

overrule to set aside an earlier court decision, done by statute or by a higher court. The overruling of a judgment on APPEAL is called REVERSAL OF JUDGMENT. *See* PRECEDENT.

owner-occupier a person who occupies a dwelling as the owner or as LESSEE under a long TENANCY. The term also refers to an owner who lived in the dwelling before letting it on an assured or regulated tenancy.

ownership the right to exclusive use, possession or disposal of property, subject only to the rights of anybody having superior title and to any restrictions imposed by law or by agreement with a third party.

P

pact an agreement or promise between states. *See* TREATY.

pain and suffering pain, shock and embarrassment due to disfigurement caused by personal injury. An award of DAMAGES may be made, based on the degree to which the injured party experiences these feelings.

palatine courts courts in the 'counties palatine' (Durham, Lancashire and Cheshire), abolished between 1830 and 1971.

palm print an impression of the palm of the hand, used for purposes of identification.

paramount superior; a term used to denote superior title in land law.

paramount clause in a BILL OF LADING, a clause that incorporates responsibilities, liabilities, rights and immunities (the so-called *Hague Rules*).

parcel (1) a plot of land. (2) in conveyancing, the clause that describes the property.

pardon the extinguishing of a punishment through exercise of the PREROGATIVE OF MERCY or by Act of Parliament. A pardon excuses a misdemeanour but does not quash a conviction.

parent father or mother, and used to refer to step-parents as well as natural parents.

parental responsibility the duties and powers one has towards children under the age of 18. Responsibility falls on both married parents; on the mother if the parents are unmarried, although the father can apply to the court for responsibility. Parental responsibility can be awarded by the court to persons other than the natural or step-parents. *See* IN LOCO PARENTIS.

parents' liability parents are not usually responsible for a child's TORT, except if the child is employed by its parent and the tort is committed in the course of that employment, or the tort is committed because of a parent's NEGLIGENCE.

parking offence an offence involving the positioning of a motor vehicle in contravention of statutory restrictions. Such offences, which include parking in a restricted area and parking within the roadmarks at a pedestrian crossing, are punishable by fine. *See also* OBSTRUCTION.

parliamentary counsel civil servants who are also BARRISTERS and who draft government bills, amendments to bills, etc.

parliamentary privilege rights and immunities enjoyed by members of the House of Commons and the House of Lords. They are designed to allow members to carry out their duties unhindered and free from undue influence. There is a Committee of Privileges to consider questions arising about privilege. Among rights enjoyed is freedom of speech in debate and freedom from arrest or molestation.

parol verbal, oral.

parol contract the same as a SIMPLE CONTRACT.

parole, also known as **release on licence**, the early, conditional release of a prisoner following assessment by the Parole

Board. Prisoners given specific sentences are automatically eligible for parole after a certain period of time. A prisoner can be recalled to prison during his or her period of parole; a prisoner who commits an offence during the parole period may have to serve the outstanding part of the original sentence.

parol evidence the same as ORAL EVIDENCE.

parol evidence rule the rule that the contents of a document cannot be altered by ORAL EVIDENCE, unless FRAUD or a MISTAKE is alleged.

parol lease a LEASE, made orally rather than in writing and not by DEED. It becomes effective immediately and is for a period of less than three years, and at full market RENT.

partial loss loss of part of property under the terms of a marine insurance policy.

particular estate an estate granted from a larger estate. It is given for a particular period of time and less than a FEE SIMPLE.

particular lien the right to retain goods until all charges have been paid and the claims of the possessor have been satisfied.

particulars the information relating to PLEADINGS needed by the other party, especially if an allegation is ambiguous or if insufficient detail is given. *See* SURPRISE.

particular tenant the owner of a PARTICULAR ESTATE.

parties (1) persons who are involved together in LITIGATION. (2) persons who join together in a transaction, such as a CONTRACT or DEED.

partition (1) the distribution or division of territory under separate administration. (2) in land law, the division of possession of land in common ownership into separate parts.

partition of chattels the division of chattels in undivided shares among the co-owners, who then individually own their shares absolutely.

partnership an arrangement of two or more persons conducting a business with the aim of making a profit. Partners are liable for debts, and a partnership (unlike a company) is not regarded in law as a 'person'. A partnership may be dissolved by the court, voluntarily by the parties, or by death. *See* LIMITED PARTNERSHIP.

part payment rule a debt cannot be satisfied by the payment of a lesser sum on the due date.

part performance an equitable doctrine that a CONTRACT that has to be evidenced in writing but is not in writing can still be enforced if a party to the contract fulfils some part of it.

party costs until 1986, the basis of taxing costs such that the loser was required to meet all reasonable and necessary costs incurred by the winner in an action.

passing off a TORT involving misleading the public into believing that one's business is that of another. Examples include packaging and marketing goods so that they look like those of another manufacturer. Passing off is actionable even if there was no intention to deceive.

passive trust *see* BARE TRUST.

passport a document issued to UK citizens and British protected persons to provide evidence of the holder's nationality and intended to ensure safe passage from one country to another. It is more common for a passport to be required on entering than on leaving a country. A passport can be withdrawn or revoked at any time by the government.

past consideration a form of CONSIDERATION wholly executed before a promise is made, as a person promising to pay a sum to another for a service done after, not before, the service is wholly done. It is not possible to sue on past consideration.

pasturage *see* PASTURE.

pasture the right to let one's cattle graze on another's land or on common land, known in Scotland as **pasturage**.

patent the exclusive right to use or sell in the UK only something one has discovered or invented, and to sue for infringement of patent. An application has to be prepared to persuade the Patent Office that the thing invented is new, involves some inventive step, has some industrial use and will not encourage antisocial conduct. A patent is usually granted for 20 years from the date of application and may be extended. During that time, the discoverer or inventor may assign the patent or grant licences for its use. If another person makes or sells the invention, that constitutes infringement. *See also* REVOCATION OF PATENT.

patent agent an expert who prepares an application for the granting of a PATENT.

patent ambiguity *see* AMBIGUITY.

patent defect *see* DEFECT.

patentee a person to whom a PATENT has been granted.

paternity the status of being the father of a particular child. This may be expressed as a declaration of paternity.

patrial the name that was given, before the 1983 amendment to the British Nationality Act 1981, to a person who had the right of abode in the UK.

pawn an article transferred by the owner to another as surety for a loan. *See also* PLEDGE.

pawnbroker a person who is licensed to take goods in PAWN and to lend money at a specified rate of interest.

pay as you earn (PAYE) a system under which income tax is paid by wage and salary earners. Tax due is deducted at source, i.e. from the wage or salary paid. The employer is responsible for accounting to the Inland Revenue.

payee a person to whom a BILL OF EXCHANGE is payable.

payment by post the settlement of a debt by sending a cheque, bank notes, etc, through the post. The debt is not paid if the payment is lost in the post, unless the creditor specifically requested payment by post.

payment in due course the payment of a BILL OF EXCHANGE on or after the maturity date in good faith and without notice that the holder's title is defective.

payment into court a payment by the DEFENDANT in an action for debt or damages in an attempt to satisfy some or all of the PLAINTIFF's claims. Such payment is deposited through the Court Funds Office.

peace *see* BREACH OF THE PEACE.

pecuniary legacy a gift or gifts of cash made through the instrument of a WILL.

pedigree an ancestral line, which may apply both to humans and animals.

pedlar a person who regularly earns all or part of his or her living from selling goods carried from place to place.

peer a person entitled to membership of the House of Lords. An *hereditary peerage* may be passed from one generation to the next; a *life peerage* obtains for the lifetime of the title holder. Both hereditary and life peers and peeresses are created by the Crown on the advice of the Prime Minister.

penal servitude imprisonment with compulsory labour. It replaced transportation in 1853.

penal statute (1) a STATUTE that creates an offence. (2) a statute that provides for the recovery of penalties in civil proceedings.

penalty a clearly stated PUNISHMENT for a CRIME. *See* FIXED PENALTY.

penalty clause a stipulation in a CONTRACT that imposes a penalty for breach of contract. Usually, the penalty clause entitles the plaintiff only to the recovery of damage suffered.

penalty points *see* TOTTING UP.

pendente lite literally 'action is pending'. The court may appoint an administrator to manage a deceased person's estate that is the subject of dispute until proceedings to resolve the dispute.

pending action court proceedings that relate to land or interest in land.

peppercorn rent a nominal RENT, usually of an insignificant amount, paid to maintain a title.

per capita literally 'by heads', distribution of property among all persons entitled to a share of it.

per curiam literally 'by the court', usually abbreviated to *per cur*. The term is used to describe a decision made by the court as a whole rather than the OPINION of an individual judge.

peremptory challenge prior to 1988, a CHALLENGE TO JURY made without a reason having to be given. Since 1988, a juror so challenged may rejoin the jury but can be challenged for cause (i.e. with the reason for the challenge given).

peremptory pleas *see* PLEAS IN BAR.

perfect and imperfect rights rights recognized in law. Perfect rights can be enforced by court action; imperfect rights cannot. *See* RIGHT.

perfection of gift the properly constituted transfer of ownership of property. *See* IMPERFECT GIFT.

perfect trust *see* EXECUTED TRUST.

performance (1) the completion of an act. (2) an act that discharges a CONTRACT by virtue of being in exact accordance with the terms of it.

performance bond a BOND given as a guarantee that a party will fulfil the terms of a contract, and generally payable unconditionally.

perils of the sea in marine insurance, damage, beyond normal wear and tear, caused at sea by violent winds or storms, striking submerged rocks, or collision.

per incuriam literally 'through want of care'. A court decision that constitutes a MISTAKE OF LAW, e.g. because it does not apply a statute or ignores a binding PRECEDENT.

periodical payments regular payments that a court may order a husband to make to his wife for a specified length of time.

periodic tenancy a TENANCY that continues beyond the original fixed period for similar subsequent periods, until terminated.

perished goods goods that have been so damaged or destroyed that they no longer match their description. A sale of goods contract is void if, unknown to the vendor, goods perished before the contract was made. It is also void if goods perished after the contract was made, but *see* TRANSFER OF RISK.

perjury the offence of knowingly making a false statement when sworn as a WITNESS. Perjury is punishable by a fine or imprisonment. *See* SUBORNATION.

per minas literally 'by menaces'.

permissive waste damage or deterioration to property that results from the failure of a TENANT to maintain the property.

perpetual injunction an INJUNCTION that is granted after the hearing of an action.

perpetuating testimony a procedure that enables EVIDENCE to be recorded for possible future use, where there is a danger that it might be lost, e.g. through the death of a WITNESS.

persistent offender the old name for a person whose previous criminal record rendered him or her liable to a prison sentence longer than the maximum prescribed for the offence of which he or she is convicted (an EXTENDED SENTENCE, abolished 1991).

person (1) a 'natural' person, an individual human being with rights and duties. (2) an 'artificial', 'fictitious' or 'juristic' person, such as a company or corporation to which the law attributes personality.

personal action an action that seeks remedies against persons. *See* REAL ACTION.

personal credit agreement an arrangement under the terms of which a creditor provides a debtor with credit of any amount.

personal information information about a living person, such that the person is identifiable from the information held. It may include the opinions about the person of the authority holding the information.

personal injuries any disease or impairment of a person's physical or mental capacity, which may be the basis of a claim for DAMAGES.

personality the sum of a person's legal rights and duties, known as **legal personality**; the rights and duties of a corporate body are called **corporate personality**.

personal property or **personalty** anything in ownership other than land, but including a leasehold interest.

personal protection order a court order that protects a spouse or child of the marriage from violence.

personal representative the EXECUTOR OF ADMINISTRATOR of the estate of a deceased person, appointed by the terms of a WILL or the rules of INTESTACY.

personal service the leaving of a document in LITIGATION with the person on whom it is being served, and informing that person of its nature.

personalty *see* PERSONAL PROPERTY.

persona non grata literally 'unacceptable person', the term used to describe a diplomat whose presence is unacceptable to the country to which he or she is accredited.

personation the offence of pretending or claiming to be another person for improper reasons, such as voting in place of someone else in an election or impersonating a member of a JURY.

person in authority the status required of a person hearing a CONFESSION. This includes a PROSECUTOR, a police officer and a MAGISTRATE.

person of unsound mind one suffering from a mental disorder.

per stirpes literally 'by the roots'. In cases of INTESTACY, or when beneficiaries predecease a TESTATOR, the distribution of property among those of the next generation entitled to share in it.

persuading to murder the offence of persuading a person to MURDER someone else. It is punishable by a sentence of up to life imprisonment.

persuasive authority a non-binding form of PRECEDENT, which a court may or may not apply as it thinks fit. Such authority is usually in the form of a decision of an inferior court or a court in a different legal system.

perverse verdict the VERDICT of a JURY that is against the EVIDENCE given or the judge's direction on a point of law.

perverting the course of justice an action that tends and is intended to obstruct or distort the administration of justice. Examples include giving false EVIDENCE in order to mislead a court, making false statements to the police, destroying evidence, threatening witnesses and attempting to influence jurors.

petition a written application for a legal remedy, such as in a DIVORCE petition, a BANKRUPTCY petition or a PETITION FOR WINDING UP of a company.

petition for winding up an application that a company be wound up by the court. *See* WINDING UP.

petition of right a procedure for obtaining restitution from the Crown, effectively from the government or other administrative body. Petitions of right were made ordinary actions by the Crown Proceedings Act 1947.

petty larceny the offence of stealing property worth less than 12 pence. Stealing goods worth more than 12 pence was *grand larceny*. The distinction was abolished in 1827.

philanthropic purposes a term used to describe the motive for making gifts, with a wider intention of bestowing benefit than in making charitable gifts.

phone tapping *see* ELECTRONIC SURVEILLANCE.

picketing attending one's place of work with the intention of peacefully and lawfully persuading others not to work, or of exchanging information, in the furtherance of a TRADE DISPUTE. Where the premises of an employer who is not an immediate party to the dispute are picketed, it is known as *secondary picketing*. Lawful pickets enjoy some forms of immunity but may be guilty of offences such as OBSTRUCTION and PUBLIC NUISANCE.

pickpocket one who steals from another's person (as opposed to another's premises, motor vehicle, etc).

piracy (1) an armed attack on the HIGH SEAS that is not an act of war. It is properly called piracy *jure gentium* ('piracy at common law') and was made a capital offence in 1837. Piracy may also be committed against an aircraft. (2) the term is also used to refer to INFRINGEMENT of COPYRIGHT, usually when it occurs in another country.

piscary the right to catch fish from water that belongs to someone else.

place of safety order another term for an EMERGENCY PROTECTION ORDER.

plaint a written statement of the cause of an action.

plaintiff a person who brings an action in court to seek redress from another, called the DEFENDANT.

planning permission official consent given by a local planning authority for the erection or alteration of buildings. When granted, it may be conditional or unconditional.

plant *see* MACHINERY AND PLANT.

plc an abbreviation of 'public limited company'. *See* PUBLIC COMPANY.

plea (1) a response, by or on behalf of an ACCUSED person, in the form of a formal statement in court, to the charges made against him or her. (2) in a common-law action, a defendant's answer to a plaintiff's declaration.

plea bargaining a procedure by which a DEFENDANT agrees to plead guilty to an offence in return for the dropping by the PROSECUTION of other charges or to secure a more lenient SENTENCE. Certain principles apply, including that the defendant must not falsely plead guilty and must not be persuaded by his or her COUNSEL to plead guilty.

plead to put forward a PLEA.

pleading guilty by post a procedure that involves pleading guilty to certain minor offences by letter rather than appearing in court. It applies only to SUMMARY OFFENCES and is commonly used in relation to less serious motoring offences.

pleading in the alternative in civil cases, including two or more inconsistent allegations in PLEADINGS and leaving it to the court to decide which it finds well-founded.

pleadings in civil actions, formal written statements in which one party to an action states the facts of the allegation against his or her opponent. Pleadings are usually drafted by COUNSEL and do not include the EVIDENCE that is to be offered to prove the facts. *See also* AMENDMENT OF PLEADINGS; CLOSE OF PLEADINGS; EXCHANGE OF PLEADINGS; SUBSEQUENT PLEADINGS.

pleas in bar, also known as **peremptory pleas**, in a trial on indictment, a PLEA that the indictment should not be proceeded with on special grounds. *See AUTREFOIS ACQUIT; AUTREFOIS CONVICT*.

pledge a surety; transfer of chattels as security for the payment of a debt. *See* PAWN.

plene administravit literally 'he has fully administered', a DEFENCE by the EXECUTOR OR ADMINISTRATOR of a deceased person's estate, who is being sued for the testator's debts of which he or she had no knowledge, that he or she has fully administered the estate and nothing remains.

plenipotentiary a person in whom full powers to act have been vested. It is applied, for example, to ambassadors and other representatives of the Sovereign.

poaching taking game or fish from private land without permission and trespassing for this purpose. There are a number of statutory offences that do not amount to theft, such as taking, injuring or killing deer and the poaching of endangered species.

poinding in Scotland, the enforcement of payment by applying to the court to sell the debtor's goods of sufficient value to cover the debt and expenses incurred in the process.

poison a substance that when administered is injurious to health or life. It is an offence to administer a poison to any person so as to endanger life or inflict bodily harm, and this can incur a sentence on conviction of life imprisonment.

police authorities committees that control the work of regular POLICE FORCES. In England and Wales, the committees are made up of local councillors and MAGISTRATES. The Home Secretary is the authority for the Metropolitan Police Force in London, and the Court of Common Council for the City of London Police Force.

police cadet a person who is undergoing training to be a POLICE OFFICER.

Police Complaints Authority a body established in 1984 to investigate complaints against the police. Reports are submitted by chief constables and the Authority can require disciplinary charges to be made.

police force a group of POLICE OFFICERS provided by a POLICE AUTHORITY for a specific area of the country. There are 52 forces in England, Wales and Scotland.

police officer a person who serves the Crown as an officer of the peace. He or she is not technically a servant of the Crown nor an employee of a local authority, but independent.

police protection order a court order authorizing the police to remove to secure accommodation a child considered to be at risk of harm. A child may be held in police protection for only up to 72 hours.

police right to question *see* QUESTIONING BY POLICE.

political asylum refuge offered to a person subject to UK immigration control on the grounds that he or she would be at risk of persecution for religious, racial or political reasons in the country from which he or she arrived.

political offence an offence that it is argued is political in nature. An offender may have protection from EXTRADITION.

pollution making something unclean. The term is most commonly used in relation to the environment, and there are a number of offences that involve releasing substances to the detriment of the health of humans and other living organisms.

polygamy having more than one spouse. Some systems permit polygamy. In the UK a polygamous marriage is void unless neither spouse was resident in the UK when the marriage was contracted.

pornography obscene material, such as books, magazines, films, etc. *See* OBSCENE PUBLICATIONS.

portion money or other property left to a child by its parent or a person *IN LOCO PARENTIS* and intended to make some form of long-term provision and to 'establish' him or her in life.

positive law legal rules formulated and imposed by the state. *See also* NATURAL LAW.

possession a degree of control over property, which is actual; the right to receive RENT and profit. *See also* QUIET POSSESSION.

possession of drugs (1) the offence of having a controlled drug in one's possession. (2) the offence of having a controlled drug, whether lawfully or unlawfully, in one's possession with the intention of supplying it to another person in breach of the Misuse of Drugs Act 1971.

possessory lien a type of LIEN when someone in possession of goods sells them to another in ignorance of the lien of a third party.

possessory title an interim registration of land in cases where the applicant is unable at present to establish title, e.g. by DEED. Possessory title does not protect the possessor from any subsisting rights or title.

possibility in land law, an interest that will arise when an uncertain future event occurs. A *bare possibility* describes the expectation of inheriting land under the terms of a WILL and confers no rights or interest; a possibility coupled with an interest may be transferred by will or by DEED.

possibility of reverter an interest in land held by one who has conveyed the land to another until such time as a specific event, which is not certain to happen, occurs. Legal estate reverts to the grantor automatically when this event occurs.

post-dated cheque a cheque bearing a date after the actual date on which it was drawn.

posthumous child a child born after the death of its father.

post-mortem literally 'after death'. The examination of a body to establish the cause of death, also known as an **autopsy**. It may be ordered by a CORONER. *See* INQUEST.

postnuptial agreement an agreement between married partners made after the marriage ceremony. A settlement made before the marriage ceremony is called an *ante-nuptial agreement.*

power the authority, as opposed to a duty, to do or not to do something. Where an action goes beyond the scope of the power, or the power affects the rights of others, it is invalid or can be challenged in the courts.

power of appointment the power given to a person to dispose of property belonging to someone else. Such power is usually vested by SETTLEMENT or TRUST.

power of attorney the authority given by a person to a nominated other to act for him or her. Enduring power of attorney cannot be revoked in the event of the subsequent incapacity of the grantor.

power of sale (1) the right of a TENANT FOR LIFE to sell land for the best obtainable price. (2) the right of a mortgagee, subject to certain restrictions, to sell mortgaged property if the mortgagor has not repaid the debt by the contractual date.

power of search the right to search persons or property vested in the police and customs officers or other officials for the purpose of procuring evidence for a prosecution. Powers of search are conferred by various statutes. *See* SEARCH WARRANT.

practice formal PROCEDURE that relates to court PROCEEDINGS.

Practice Directions notes published in law reports that express the views of judges and others on matters of practice and PROCEDURE. They have no statutory authority. *See* RULES OF COURT.

practising certificate an annual certificate that a SOLICITOR must hold in order to practise. It is issued by the Law Society in England and Wales and in Scotland by the Law Society of Scotland.

praecipe literally 'command'. Formerly, a WRIT that ordered a person to perform an act or show reason for non-performance.

preamble the opening parts of a statute, which explains its purpose and supposed effects. It may be useful for reference if the statute itself proves ambiguous.

precarious possession a type of POSSESSION, not by right but by the will of another person.

precatory trust *see* PRECATORY WORDS.

precatory words words that, in a document gifting property, express a wish or request that the receiver will dispose of it in a particular manner. If there is sufficient certainty that there was a wish to create a TRUST, this is referred to as a 'precatory trust'.

precedent a court decision or judgment that is used as the basis for subsequent decisions and judgments. They are usually binding on lower courts when made in higher courts. The principles of the decision, known as *RATIO DECIDENDI*, are binding; other parts may not be.

precept a command or written order. In relation to the payment of rates, it demands that an authority levy rates for the benefit of another authority.

predecessor in land law, a person from whom succession to property is derived. Examples include a mortgagee (who had exercised POWER OF SALE) and a TESTATOR.

pre-emption the right to purchase, e.g. land, before anyone else; the right of 'first refusal'.

preference (1) the right, now abolished, of a PERSONAL REPRESENTATIVE to pay one CREDITOR before any others. (2) the favouring by a DEBTOR or an insolvent company of one creditor over others.

preference shares shares in a company that rank for payment before ORDINARY SHARES but after DEBENTURES.

preferential debts in cases of BANKRUPTCY, types of liability that must be paid before others. These include debts to employees.

preferment (1) bringing a BILL OF INDICTMENT before a court. (2) bringing a charge against a person.

pregnancy *see* MATERNITY RIGHTS.

pregnancy *per alium* pregnancy by a person other than the woman's husband. A marriage may be voidable if, at the time of marriage, the wife was pregnant by another man.

pre-hearing assessment an examination of the likely success of an application to an INDUSTRIAL TRIBUNAL. A pre-hearing may be requested by either party or by the tribunal itself. Costs may be awarded if the application has little chance of success but is not withdrawn.

pre-incorporation contract a CONTRACT made between a person and someone acting as AGENT or TRUSTEE for a company that has not yet been formed. The latter is personally liable on such a contract.

prejudice preconceived judgment. The writer of a document may use the words 'without prejudice' as protection against any interpretation of the contents as an admission of liability. *See also* UNFAIR PREJUDICE.

preliminary enquiry or **preliminary investigation** the investigation by a MAGISTRATE of a case before it goes for trial in a higher court. The prosecution must convince the magistrate that it can show a *PRIMA FACIE* case against the accused, who is then committed for trial. The defendant is discharged if the prosecution cannot do so.

preliminary point of law a point of law considered by the judge when there is a plea of not guilty and before the jury is empanelled, and when the point of law will be decisive.

premises (1) property such as land and buildings. (2) the parts of a DEED that set out the names of the parties and list the property to be transferred.

premium (1) a periodic payment made to keep up a contract of INSURANCE. (2) a lump sum paid by a TENANT when a LEASE is granted or renewed. (3) a reward.

preparatory hearing in cases of SERIOUS FRAUD, a hearing before a judge to identify and, if necessary, explain issues likely to arise and prove complex.

prerogative *see* ROYAL PREROGATIVE.

prerogative of mercy the power of the Crown, on the advice of the Home Secretary, to PARDON an offence or commute a SENTENCE.

prerogative orders *see* *CERTIORARI*; *MANDAMUS*; PROHIBITION.

prescribed limits in relation to motoring offences, the ratio of alcohol to blood, breath or urine laid down as the legal permitted maximum.

prescription the acquisition or extinguishing of rights through the passage of time, *acquisitive prescription* and *negative prescription* respectively. One can acquire an EASEMENT from continuous use over a long period of time; rights may be lost if the owner fails to exercise them over a similarly long period.

presentment the presenting of a BILL OF EXCHANGE for acceptance or payment.

presents in relation to a DEED, the term refers to the document itself.

preservation order in planning law, an order relating to the preservation of a LISTED BUILDING or any building of special historical or architectural interest that is in danger of being altered or demolished. Such an order can also apply to trees.

presiding judge a HIGH COURT judge appointed to supervise circuits in England and Wales.

presumption an assumption that is made until evidence proves otherwise. The law requires certain presumptions to be made. *See* PRESUMPTION OF INNOCENCE.

presumption concerning sexual incapacity until 1993, the rule that a boy under the age of 14 was incapable of sexual intercourse.

presumption of accuracy the assumption that a mechanical instrument, such as a speed gauge, was functioning correctly at the time of an incident under investigation.

presumption of continuance the assumption that a given state of affairs has continued for some time.

presumption of death the presumption that a person has died. A decree of DIVORCE may be granted if a spouse has been missing and has not been heard of for seven years. A subsequent remarriage remains valid even if the lost spouse later reappears.

presumption of due execution the presumption that a WILL has been properly executed in the absence of any reliable evidence that it has not.

presumption of innocence the presumption that a person accused of a crime is innocent until the prosecution has proved beyond reasonable doubt that he or she is guilty.

presumption of lawful origin the presumption that a person in possession of property is its rightful owner.

presumption of legitimacy the presumption that a child born of lawfully wedded parents is legitimate.

presumption of marriage validity the presumption that a marriage is valid where there is evidence of a lawful marriage ceremony followed by cohabitation.

presumption of negligence *see* RES IPSA LOQUITUR.

presumption of sanity the presumption that a person charged with committing a criminal offence was sane when the crime was committed. *See* INSANITY.

pre-trial review the preliminary consideration of an action to be heard in the county court. EVIDENCE may be presented by AFFIDAVIT.

previous convictions in both civil and criminal cases, evidence that the accused or a witness has been previously convicted of an offence is inadmissible, unless ruled relevant or classified as SIMILAR-FACT EVIDENCE.

previous statements statements made by a witness on an earlier occasion inconsistent with his or her present testimony. Except in certain circumstances, such a statement, or the fact that it was made, is not admissible.

price the amount to be paid by the consumer for goods or services, accommodation or facilities.

price-sensitive information facts about the financial status of a business not known to the public at large and used by the holder of the information to his or her advantage. *See* INSIDER DEALING.

prima facie literally 'first appearance', 'on the face of it'.

***prima facie* case** a case in which there is enough evidence in favour of a party to prove his or her case.

***prima facie* evidence**, also known as **presumptive evidence**, evidence that, although not conclusive, offers sufficient proof of a fact; evidence that is sufficient to relieve a party of the BURDEN OF PROOF.

primary evidence evidence that by its nature does not suggest that better evidence is available. *See* SECONDARY EVIDENCE.

primary facts facts observed by witnesses or provided by documents and considered to be proved. Inferences from the facts may be challenged.

primogeniture a system, abolished in 1925, by which preference in inheritance was given to an eldest son and his children.

principal (1) the person who actually commits a crime. A person who aids or abets is known as the *secondary party*. (2) the person on whose behalf an AGENT acts. (3) a sum of money lent or invested.

principle of legality *see NULLUM CRIMEN SINE LEGE.*

priority notice a notice that registers a person's title to land and prevents, for a limited period, anyone else registering title.

priority of assignment the order in which two or more ASSIGNMENTS take effect, determined by the date on which the notice of assignment was received.

priority of mortgages the rule that determines the order in which two or more mortgages on the same property take effect. Priority is determined by the order in which the mortgages were registered.

priority of debts where a deceased person's estate is insolvent, the court's power to administer the estate.

priority of time the rule that an earlier interest generally prevails over a later competing interest.

prisoner a person lawfully held in CUSTODY in a prison or in police detention after being charged with an offence, or having been convicted and sentenced.

privacy an individual's right to be left alone. Although not a statutory right, privacy is an element in certain other protections.

private Act of Parliament an Act that is not accepted by the court as a matter of general knowledge. Most Acts are *public Acts* and are of general application.

private company a company that may not offer its shares to the general public. It may be limited or unlimited, and have one member or any number of members. *See* PUBLIC COMPANY.

private defence a defence to an action in TORT that a person acting in defence of self or property took reasonable measures and is not liable for the tort.

private international law the part of the law that deals with cases where a foreign element is present and where it must be decided which court has jurisdiction. Also known as *conflict of laws*.

private law the parts of the law concerned with individuals' duties and rights which are not of direct concern to the state, such as contract law and family law. *See* PUBLIC LAW.

private Members' Bills Bills introduced by private Members of the House of Commons or House of Lords and not by the government.

private nuisance conduct that interferes with rights over land. *See also* PUBLIC NUISANCE.

private prosecution the prosecution by an individual or individuals rather than the Crown of an indictable offence.

privatization the transfer of the assets of state-owned enterprises to the private sector, usually through the creation of a PUBLIC COMPANY and the issue of SHARES.

privilege (1) a special right or immunity from legal proceedings enjoyed by individuals or bodies (*see* PARLIAMENTARY PRIVILEGE). (2) justification for a refusal to answer a question or, in a 'claim of privilege', to produce documents in the course of a court action. *See also* ABSOLUTE PRIVILEGE; QUALIFIED PRIVILEGE.

privileged communication (1) a confidential communication, e.g. between husband and wife, or between solicitor and client, which may not be offered in evidence without the consent of the owner of the privilege. (2) an official communication that may not be offered in evidence on the grounds that to do so would be against the public interest. (3) a communication that may contain defamatory statements (*see* DEFAMATION) but is protected by ABSOLUTE PRIVILEGE.

privileged will the right of a person on active military service to make an informal WILL, i.e. one not made following the normal formalities, which will be held to be valid.

privilege of witness the right of a WITNESS not to answer certain types of question, e.g. self-incriminatory questions or questions endangering the security of the state. A witness enjoys immunity from action for DEFAMATION while answering questions on OATH.

privity the relationship that exists between people as a result of their participating together in a transaction.

privity of contract the relationship that exists between the parties to a CONTRACT. One of the principles that applies is that only a party to the contract may sue on it.

privity of estate the relationship that exists between LANDLORD and TENANT or LESSOR and LESSEE.

privy being a participant in an act; being in PRIVITY to another person or body.

Privy Council a body with limited statutory powers that advises the Sovereign and is headed by the Lord President of the Council. The 390 members of the Council include members of the Royal Family, Cabinet Ministers and the Speaker of the House of Commons, as well as people honoured for public service. *See* ORDERS OF COUNCIL; ORDERS IN COUNCIL.

prize courts courts that decide matters relating to the seizing, in times of war, of ships, aircraft, etc, at sea or in port, in accordance with INTERNATIONAL LAW.

probate a court document evidencing the authority of the EXECUTOR of a WILL. The court must 'grant probate' when a will is contested.

probate action court proceedings for the granting or revocation of PROBATE and to determine whether or not a WILL is valid.

Probate, Divorce and Admiralty Division formerly, a division of the HIGH COURT and now known as the Family Division. Admiralty jurisdiction was moved to the QUEEN'S BENCH DIVI-

SION and contentious probate jursidiction to the CHANCERY DIVISION in 1970.

probate rules rules that regulate the practice and procedure of the HIGH COURT in relation to non-contentious probate matters.

probation the placing of an offender over the age of 16 under the supervision of a PROBATION OFFICER for a period of six months to three years. The offender must be willing to be bound by the PROBATION ORDER, to be of good behaviour during the probation period, and not to commit other offences.

probation centre a non-residential facility provided with the approval of the Secretary of State to assist with the rehabilitation of a person subject to a PROBATION ORDER.

probationer a person under supervision because of the serving of a PROBATION ORDER.

probation hostel a residential facility for persons required to reside there by a PROBATION ORDER.

probation officer an official appointed to supervise persons bound by a PROBATION ORDER and to assist in their rehabilitation. Such an officer may also be required to advise the court regarding the treatment of probationers.

probation order a court order, imposed with the consent of an offender, placing him or her (for between six months and three years) under the supervision of a PROBATION OFFICER.

procedure the manner in which judicial PROCEEDINGS are conducted. *See* RULES OF COURT.

proceedings the conducting of business before a court. *See* INTERLOCUTORY PROCEEDINGS; STAY OF PROCEEDINGS.

process (1) a SUMMONS requiring the attendance in court of the DEFENDANT. (2) the way in which something operates. *See also* ABUSE OF PROCESS.

Procurator Fiscal in Scotland, a court officer, appointed by the LORD ADVOCATE, who initiates preliminary investigations into criminal cases.

procurement (1) the offence of procuring a woman, with threats or intimidation, to have unlawful sexual intercourse. (2) procuring a woman under the age of 21 to have sexual intercourse with a third party. (3) procuring a woman for the purposes of PROSTITUTION.

procuring breach of contract, also known as **inducing breach of contract**, the TORT of persuading a person to break the terms of his or her contract with a third party. The party who suffers loss may sue the procuror.

production of documents the production, by order of the court, of books and documents for inspection. *See also* DISCOVERY AND INSPECTION OF DOCUMENTS.

product liability under consumer protection legislation, the liability of the manufacturer or importer of defective goods, including the liability for death or injury caused because the goods were defective. A claim for damage to property can only be made if the damage caused exceeds £275 in value.

professional misconduct behaviour by a member of a profession deemed by the profession's governing body to be below the standard expected of him or her.

profits *à prendre* the right to take something from another person's land or to graze animals on it. The profits may take one of several different forms and may be held by one person or several.

prohibited degrees of relationships the relationships between family members that prohibit marriage. *See also* INCEST.

prohibited steps orders in the care of children, court orders that prohibit specified acts with regard to children without the court's consent. *See also* SECTION 8 ORDERS.

prohibited weapon a weapon designed and manufactured for military and not civilian use. The category includes automatic firearms. It is an offence to produce, buy, sell or possess a prohibited weapon without permission.

prohibition a HIGH COURT order (known as a **prerogative order**) that an inferior court should not proceed with a course of action, e.g. hearing an action that is outside its jurisdiction.

prohibition notice under the Health and Safety at Work Act 1974, a notice served by an inspector to the effect that activities that, in his or her opinion, constitute a risk to health and safety must cease until remedied.

prohibitory injunction a court order that prohibits the continuing performance of a wrongful act. Failure to comply may constitute CONTEMPT OF COURT.

prolixity unnecessary length or repetition in PLEADINGS or AFFIDAVITS. Someone engaging in prolixity may be liable for costs incurred as a result of it.

promise an undertaking given, which is only legally binding if in the form of a CONTRACT or COVENANT.

promissory estoppel *see* ESTOPPEL.

promissory note an unconditional promise to pay a sum of money at a specified time or on demand, made in writing and signed by the promiser.

promoter (1) a person who initiates a PRIVATE BILL. (2) a person who is involved in the formation of a company and who has a FIDUCIARY RELATIONSHIP to the company.

proof the method by which the existence or non-existence of a fact is established to the satisfaction of the court. Means include EVIDENCE, PRESUMPTION and TESTIMONY.

proof before answer in Scotland, the hearing of the facts of a case before any legal arguments. It is commonly used in cases of NEGLIGENCE.

proof beyond reasonable doubt the standard of proof that leaves no more than a remote possibility of doubt and that is required in criminal proceedings. If the JURY entertains a reasonable doubt, it may not deliver a VERDICT of guilty. *See* BURDEN OF PROOF; STANDARDS OF PROOF.

proof of age direct evidence or documentary evidence (such as a birth certificate) of a person's date of birth.

proof of birth proof of someone's birth, usually through the production of a birth certificate combined with evidence that the person in question is the same person as that mentioned in the birth certificate.

proof of handwriting establishing the authenticity of a person's handwriting, either through that person's own evidence or that of someone who witnessed his or her writing of the document in question. An EXPERT WITNESS may be called.

proof of marriage establishing that a valid marriage took place, usually by producing a marriage certificate and from identification of the parties.

proper law of contract in PRIVATE INTERNATIONAL LAW, that which denotes which system of law governs a CONTRACT. It is usually the system that it was the parties' intention should apply.

property something that can be owned. *Real property* refers to land; *personal property* to all other kinds. *Tangible property* has a physical existence; *intangible property* consists of CHOSES IN ACTION and INCORPOREAL HEREDITAMENTS.

property adjustment order a court order affecting the rights of ownership of property of either spouse following a decree of DIVORCE, NULLITY or JUDICIAL SEPARATION.

property in goods title or ownership in CHATTELS.

property register *see* LAND REGISTRATION.

proponent (1) the party, such as the PROSECUTION or the PLAINTIFF, who must first raise an action. (2) the party who bears the evidential and legal BURDEN OF PROOF.

propositus (1) that person immediately concerned. (2) an ancestor from whom descent is traced. (3) a TESTATOR.

proprietary estoppel *see* ESTOPPEL.

proprietor a person who enjoys TITLE to PROPERTY.

proscribed organization under the Prevention of Terrorism Act, an organization or association prohibited because its activities are considered harmful and connected with TERRORISM. It is an offence to belong to a proscribed organization, to raise funds for it or to make contributions to it. It is not an offence to speak publicly in its support.

prosecution (1) the instituting of legal proceedings, especially criminal proceedings, in the courts. (2) the term used to refer to the party pursuing such proceedings. *See also* DEFENCE; PRIVATE PROSECUTION.

prosecutor the person who institutes criminal proceedings, usually in the name of the Crown.

prospectus a document that offers SHARES or DEBENTURES in a PUBLIC COMPANY.

prostitution the offering by a person of his or her body for sexual purposes in return for the payment of money. It is not itself an offence, but some activities associated with it are, including LIVING ON IMMORAL EARNINGS, PROCUREMENT and SOLICITING.

protected child a child whom someone wants to adopt. An adoption agency is responsible for supervising such a child. If there is no agency involved, the local authority has responsibility for the child's supervision.

protected furnished tenancy a PROTECTED TENANCY under the terms of which a substantial part of the RENT paid is in respect of furnishings.

protected goods goods that have been sold under a hire purchase or extended credit agreement and for which the purchaser has paid a third or more of the debt. If the purchaser is then in default, the goods can be recovered only by court order.

protected occupancy in the renting of agricultural dwellings, the right of a TENANT to occupy a TIED COTTAGE and to enjoy protection similar to that afforded by a PROTECTED TENANCY.

protected person a head of state or head of government, as well as several other categories of office-holder, entitled under international law to protection from personal injury when outside the country in which he or she holds office.

protected shorthold tenancy prior to 1988, a PROTECTED TENANCY of one to five years' duration. It was replaced by the ASSURED SHORTHOLD TENANCY.

protected state, also known as a **protectorate**, a state that has a considerable measure of autonomy (especially over internal affairs) but is under the protection of another state.

protected tenancy a TENANCY relating to a separate dwelling; the tenant has a right to pay a fair rent and enjoy SECURITY OF TENTURE. In 1988, it was replaced by the ASSURED TENANCY.

Protection and Indemnity Association in marine insurance, an arrangement in which shipowners make contributions to the Association and in return the Association meets the cost of certain liabilities not usually covered.

protection order a court order made following an application by an owner or creditor for the protection of property from damage pending the determination of proceedings under the Consumer Credit Act 1974.

protective award in cases of REDUNDANCY, an award by an INDUSTRIAL TRIBUNAL for continuing remuneration to an employee or employees made redundant when the employer has failed to follow the prescribed consultation procedure.

protective trust a TRUST for the lifetime of the beneficiary or until a specified event occurs. In the event of the beneficiary's BANKRUPTCY, the income is applied at the discretion of the trustees.

protest a document issued by a NOTARY as evidence of the DISHONOUR OF A BILL OF EXCHANGE; when payment is made 'under protest', the payer does not agree that he or she is liable to pay.

protocol (1) an original draft of a document. (2) an agreement between states that is less formal than a TREATY. (3) minutes of a meeting.

provable debt a debt that a creditor can claim from the assets of someone in BANKRUPTCY. *See also* NON-PROVABLE DEBT.

provident benefits payments made under union rules to a member who is sick, incapacitated or unemployed, or as superannuation.

proving a will the process of obtaining PROBATE of a WILL.

provisional damages a form of DAMAGES awarded to a plaintiff whose present condition may lead to a more serious condition in the future, when the plaintiff may return to the court to apply for further damages.

provisional liquidator a person appointed to conduct the WINDING UP of a company prior to the appointment of a LIQUIDATOR.

provisional orders orders issued by government departments that do not take effect until confirmed by Parliament.

proviso (1) a condition in a DEED upon which its validity is based. (2) a clause in a STATUTE that specifically excludes something that would otherwise have been automatically included.

provocation words or deeds that cause a person to lose self-control. It does not usually constitute a defence but may play a part in mitigation, especially in cases of serious criminal charges; e.g. MURDER may be reduced to MANSLAUGHTER.

proxy someone given the authority to act for another, e.g. to vote at a meeting. The term also applies to a document conferring such authority.

psychopathic disorder a persistent mental disorder that results in abnormally aggressive or seriously irresponsible behaviour.

Public Accounts Committee a select committee of the House of Commons that monitors government spending and investigates irregularities. It was established in 1861.

public Act of Parliament an Act that affects the public at large. Most Acts are public, but *see* PRIVATE ACT OF PARLIAMENT.

public assembly the gathering together of 20 or more persons in a public place, wholly or partly in the open air.

publication in an action for DEFAMATION, the communicating of words to a person other than the person defamed.

public benefit beneficial effects on the public at large, or an identifiable and significant group. Charitable bodies must show that their activities confer public benefit.

public body any body with responsibilities for performing duties designed to promote PUBLIC BENEFIT rather than private profit.

public company a company, limited by SHARES or by guarantee, that must comply with statutory regulations concerning registration. It can offer its shares to the public and must declare itself to be a public company. Its name must end with plc (public limited company). There is an authorized minimum capitalization. *See* PRIVATE COMPANY.

public corporation a body set up to perform a public function, which may be commercial or social. Members are appointed by a government minister.

public decency the concept of the public's susceptibility to being depraved or corrupted by something seen or heard.

public document a document prepared specifically for public use and to which the public may refer, e.g. court records.

public duties certain duties, such as sitting as a MAGISTRATE, which entitle those who perform them to time off work.

public examination an investigation in open court of the conduct and property of a debtor in cases of BANKRUPTCY. The debtor must attend and answer questions on OATH.

public house premises licensed to sell intoxicating liquor for consumption on the premises.

public law the parts of the law concerned with the powers and duties of the state. *See* PRIVATE LAW.

public limited company *see* PUBLIC COMPANY.

public mischief the former offence of acting in a way that was harmful to the community, e.g. by making hoax telephone calls. It has not been a crime since 1975.

public morals the underlying moral precepts of a society, which the courts from time to time express their discretion to enforce.

public nuisance a NUISANCE that adversely affects a large number of people and is more likely to be prosecuted on their behalf rather than by an individual.

public office any office held under the Crown, such as employment as a civil servant.

public place any HIGHWAY or place to which the public has a right of access, with or without payment. Several offences, such as being drunk and disorderly, relate to conduct 'in a public place'.

public policy the principle that no person may lawfully do something that is against the PUBLIC GOOD.

puisne judge an ordinary judge of the HIGH COURT. The term comes from Old French *puisne*, 'later born', i.e. of lesser rank.

puisne mortgage a subsequent legal MORTGAGE in which the mortgagee does not hold the title deeds to the mortgaged property.

punishment the penalty inflicted by the court on a person who has been convicted of an offence. The punishment is specified in the SENTENCE of the court. *See* CAPITAL PUNISHMENT.

punitive damages *see* EXEMPLARY DAMAGES.

pur autre vie literally 'for another life'. The term is used of a TENANT for the life of another, i.e. the tenancy is granted by A to B during the lifetime of C.

purchaser a person who acquires goods or land in exchange for payment. A purchaser of land may be a MORTGAGEE or a person to whom land has been bequeathed.

purchaser for value without notice a person who purchases land in good faith and without knowledge of any encumbrances, and is not bound by any encumbrances.

purpose trust a TRUST that is neither for the benefit of a person or persons, nor is it a charitable trust. With a few exceptions, purpose trusts are not valid.

putative father a person who is alleged to be the father of an illegitimate child. Such a person's name may appear on the birth certificate and he may be ordered by the court to make maintenance payments. *See* ILLEGITIMACY.

Q

QBD *see* QUEEN'S BENCH DIVISION.

QC *see* QUEEN'S COUNSEL.

qualified acceptance the partial or conditional acceptance of a BILL OF EXCHANGE.

qualified privilege in an action for DEFAMATION, a defence that a statement was made under PRIVILEGE and without malice, or that the person who made it was under a duty or obligation to make it. *See also* ABSOLUTE PRIVILEGE.

qualified title the ownership of registered land subject to a specified exception or qualification. Absolute, good leasehold or possessory title cannot be granted.

qualifying child in child support maintenance, a natural or adopted child below the age of 16 (or under 19 but in full-time education) who has not been married.

quango an acronym from **qu**asi-**a**utonomous **n**on-**go**vernmental organization to describe a body appointed by the government but not a government department. It usually has regulatory and operational functions. Examples include the British Council and the Monopolies and Mergers Commission.

quantum an amount, usually referring to the amount awarded in DAMAGES.

quantum meruit literally 'how much he has earned'. In cases of BREACH OF CONTRACT, the amount an injured party may be entitled to claim for work done or services provided.

quantum valebat literally 'how much it was worth'. An action to claim the value of goods that were sold without a price being agreed.

quarantine the period during which animals brought into the UK from other countries must spend in isolation, primarily designed to prevent the spread of rabies and other diseases.

quarter days four dates in the calendar used for several purposes, such as fixing dates on which RENT is due for payment. They are Lady Day (25 March), Midsummer Day (24 June), Michaelmas Day (29 September) and Christmas Day (25 December).

quash (1) to make void a conviction in an inferior court. (2) to set aside a decision pending JUDICIAL REVIEW.

quasi-contract a case in which a person has been enriched at the expense of someone else and now has an obligation ('as if by CONTRACT') to make restitution.

quasi-easement the right that a person exercises over two or more adjoining but separate pieces of land that he or she owns. As one cannot have EASEMENT over one's own land, this right is referred to 'as if it were an easement'.

quasi-entail an interest in land only good for the lifetime of a specified person. *See PUR AUTRE VIE.*

quasi ex contractu as if arising out of a CONTRACT. *See* QUASI-CONTRACT.

quasi-indorser a person who signs a BILL OF EXCHANGE, although neither the drawer nor the acceptor, and who incurs the liabilities of an indorser in due course.

quasi-judicial a process that resembles proceedings in court but that depends on the decision of, for example, an arbitrator.

Queen's Bench Division the division of the HIGH COURT with jurisdiction over civil matters relating to CONTRACT and TORT. It is presided over by the Lord Chief Justice and a staff of PUISNE JUDGES.

Queen's Counsel (QC) a senior BARRISTER who appears for or against the Crown. He or she is appointed on the recommendation of the Lord Chancellor and wears a silk gown. Becoming a QC is known as 'taking silk'.

Queen's evidence evidence given for the Crown by a co-accused person who 'turns Queen's evidence', i.e. confesses guilt and gives testimony against his or her co-accused. The judge will normally direct that such evidence may be less reliable and requires corroboration.

Queen's Proctor an office held by the TREASURY SOLICITOR, who gives legal advice to the court on problems arising in actions for DIVORCE. The Queen's Proctor can intervene to prevent a divorce being made absolute (*see* DECREE).

questioning by the police a code of practice followed by police officers who believe a person may be in a position to give useful and relevant information in the course of an investigation. It is subject to a number of restrictions. *See* RIGHT OF SILENCE.

quia timet literally 'because he fears'. An INJUNCTION sought in anticipation of a feared or threatened wrong. For such an injunction to be granted, the applicant must show good cause for fearing that the act will be committed against him or her.

quiet enjoyment the obligation of a LANDLORD in respect of a LESSEE's continued and peaceful occupation of premises.

quiet possession in the sale of goods, the right of the purchaser from interference in the enjoyment of the property transferred.

quittance a document drawn up to acknowledge the payment of a debt.

quorum a specified number of members of a body who must be present for that body to meet formally and act legally.

quotation (1) the amount suggested as a price, usually for the performance of a service. (2) the listing of a share price on the Stock Exchange.

R

racial discrimination acting against the interests of a person because of his or her ethnic origin. Various Acts have created offences, including incitement to RACIAL HATRED, discrimination in relation to the supply of goods and services, and employment.

racial hatred hatred expressed towards any group defined by colour, race, nationality or ethnic origin. Several offences relate to activities designed to stir up racial hatred.

ransom the price paid in exchange for release from captivity.

rape unlawful sexual intercourse with a woman or another man without that person's consent or by force, threat or fraud. A defendant must be shown to have known that consent was withheld, or was reckless, i.e. indifferent to whether or not consent was withheld. There are a number of other offences, including incitement to rape, aiding or abetting rape and burglary with intent to rape.

ratification (1) confirmation of an act, often cited in CONTRACT law. (2) approval of a TREATY.

ratio decidendi literally 'the reason for deciding'. *Descriptive ratio* is the reasoning by which a decision is reached; *prescriptive ratio* is reasoning that a later court is bound to follow. *See also* PRECEDENT.

rave the colloquial term for an unlicensed gathering of 100 or more people, mostly in the open air, at which loud music is played and is distressing to people in the vicinity. Under the Criminal Justice and Public Order Act 1994, the police have powers to stop a rave.

real (1) of things rather than of people. (2) relating to land.

real action an action brought for the recovery of land. *See also* PERSONAL ACTION.

real estate interests in land held by the deceased at the time of his or her death.

real evidence the form of EVIDENCE constituted by physical objects that can be shown to a JURY. *See* EXHIBIT; LABEL.

real property, also known as **realty**, (1) freehold land. (2) property that it would be possible to recover in a REAL ACTION.

real security a security charged on land; a mortgage.

realty *see* REAL PROPERTY.

reasonable doubt *see* PROOF BEYOND REASONABLE DOUBT.

reasonable financial provision the financial provision that the dependants of a deceased person may apply for in cases of INTESTACY or where no such provision is made in a WILL. 'Reasonable' describes what is required for maintenance.

reasonable force the degree of physical force that a person may use in SELF-DEFENCE or in defending his or her property.

reasonable man an ordinary, right-minded person, often cited in cases of NEGLIGENCE, where it is sought to establish what a reasonable person might expect.

rebus sic stantibus literally 'in these circumstances'. In INTERNATIONAL LAW, the doctrine that a TREATY will cease to be binding if there is a significant change in the circumstances on which it was agreed.

rebuttable presumption a PRESUMPTION that holds good only as long as there is no evidence to the contrary. PRESUMPTION OF INNOCENCE is rebutted by proof of guilt.

recall of witness the calling back of a WITNESS after the close of a party's case, which the judge may allow to hear evidence in rebuttal, i.e. which counters what has been said in CROSS-EXAMINATION.

recaption lawfully taking back one's CHATTELS from a person who has wrongfully taken them.

receipt an acknowledgment in writing that one has received money or goods.

receiver (1) a person appointed by the court to enable a creditor to obtain payment of a debt. *See* ADMINISTRATIVE RECEIVER. (2) a person appointed to protect property at risk. (3) a person who receives stolen property.

receiving prior to 1968, the offence of acquiring stolen property, now part of the offence of HANDLING. *See* FENCE.

recitals in a DEED of sale, details of the purpose and effect of the deed, and of the history of the property being transferred. A deed is valid without RECITALS.

recklessness a degree of awareness of risk when committing an offence, greater than NEGLIGENCE. The implication is that the offender unreasonably disregarded the consequences of an act, although they may have been unintended.

recognizance an undertaking to pay a specified amount to the Crown if an accused person fails to surrender to custody. *See also* BAIL. An offender may be obligated to keep the peace and be of good behaviour or forfeit a recognizance.

reconciliation settling differences between disputing parties. Attempts at reconciliation between spouses are sometimes made in actions for DIVORCE.

reconstruction of a company the transfer of the assets of a company to a new company, where shareholders receive shares or other interest in the new company.

record (1) an account of an event. (2) a document that gives an authentic account of court proceedings.

Recorders barristers or solicitors who are appointed as part-time judges to try criminal cases in the Crown Court, and who may also sit in the High Court.

recovery an action in the High Court or a county court to regain possession of land from an unlawful occupier.

recovery of costs an action to recover costs due to a solicitor for legal services. The solicitor may not sue until a month after his or her bill has been delivered to the client.

recovery of premises the right to regain possession of property of which one has been unlawfully dispossessed; the right of a court officer to enforce such a judgment. It is an offence to resist or obstruct such officers. *See* SQUATTER.

rectification the correction of a document that does not accurately reflect the intention of the parties to it. If all parties agree that rectification is required, and no third party's interests are compromised, the rectification may be made. Otherwise, application may be made to the court, which has jurisdiction to rectify.

rectification of will the correction of the terms of a WILL, which a court may authorize if satisfied that they do not fulfil the wishes of the TESTATOR, usually because of a misunderstanding or clerical error.

reddendum the clause in a LEASE that stipulates how much RENT is to be paid and when.

redeemable shares SHARES in a company that can be redeemed out of profit or a fresh share issue.

redeem up, foreclose down in the PRIORITY of mortgages, a second or later mortgagee may buy out a first or an earlier mortgagee.

redemption the repossession of mortgaged property upon payment of the debt. The right may be legal (i.e. on the exact date in the mortgage) or equitable (at a date later than that in the mortgage).

redress *see* REMEDY.

redundancy (1) the termination of a person's employment on the grounds that his or her job has ceased to exist. (2) in PLEADINGS, matters that are irrelevant.

re-engagement order an order made by an INDUSTRIAL TRIBUNAL that a former employee must be re-employed in a job similar to, but not the same as, that from which he or she has been unfairly dismissed. *See* RE-INSTATEMENT ORDER.

re-entry *see* RIGHT OF ENTRY.

re-examination examination, by the party who called him or her, of a WITNESS following the CROSS-EXAMINATION of that witness by the opposing party. In general, LEADING QUESTIONS may not be asked and new questions only with the judge's permission.

referee a person to whom a dispute is referred for an opinion. *See* OFFICIAL REFEREE.

reference the referral by a court to another court or an ARBITRATOR, of a case, or an issue raised by a case, for a decision or an opinion.

referendum the conducting of a popular vote on a proposal or question.

referential settlement a SETTLEMENT that incorporates the terms of an earlier settlement by referring to it.

refer to drawer a term used by a bank when it dishonours a cheque presented by the payee, usually because there are insufficient funds to cover the amount stated on the cheque.

refreshing memory the permission that is granted to a WITNESS to refer to a document to assist in the recollection of some detail. Generally, the document must be the witness's own, in the sense that he or she created it or supervised its creation.

refugee a person who is unable or unwilling to return to his or her native country through fear of persecution on grounds of race, religion, nationality, or membership of a social or political group.

registered company any of several types of company incorporated by REGISTRATION under the Companies Act 1985.

registered design a design that is registered at the Patent Office, which gives exclusive rights over the outward appearance of something. *See* PATENT.

registered land land to which the title is registered. *See* LAND REGISTRATION.

registered office a company's official address, which must be sent to the Registrar of Companies and which must appear on its letterhead and order forms. It is often an address different from that where its business is conducted.

register of members a register that must contain the names, addresses and shareholdings of all the members of a registered company. It must be available for public inspection during normal business hours at the company's REGISTERED OFFICE.

registrar an official appointed to keep a particular register, e.g. the Registrar of Births and Deaths.

registration as citizen a procedure that allows certain persons to become British citizens by right or at the discretion of the Secretary of State. *See also* NATURALIZATION.

registration of a company a method of forming an incorporated company. A number of documents, including a memorandum of association, articles of association and the address of the company's REGISTERED OFFICE must be lodged with the Companies Registry.

registration of birth the compulsory, official recording of a person's birth. It must be lodged with the Registrar of Births and Deaths within 42 days of the birth. It must give date and place of birth, the name and sex of the child and the names of the parents. In some circumstances, the name of an unmarried father may be entered on the birth certificate.

registration of death the compulsory, official recording of a person's death. It must be lodged with the Registrar of Births and Deaths within five days of the death (or within 14 days if written notice of the death is given to the Registrar). It must give date and place of death, the name, address, sex and occupation of the deceased, and the cause of death. A death certificate is issued by the Registrar.

registration of marriage the official recording of the details of a marriage after the marriage ceremony. It usually details the names, ages, addresses and occupations of the parties, and the names and occupations of their fathers, and the place where the marriage was solemnized.

registration of title *see* LAND REGISTRATION.

regulated agreement a consumer credit agreement or consumer hire agreement governed by the Consumer Credit Act 1974. The Act stipulates that all such agreements must be in writing, must be legible and must be signed by the debtor and the other parties.

rehabilitation period a period during which a person convicted of an offence may be considered to have spent his or her conviction and to have been 'rehabilitated'. The period is typically five to ten years and depends on the length of the SENTENCE.

re-hearing a second hearing of a case that has already been adjudicated upon, when new evidence may be introduced by either side. A re-hearing may be held when a person convicted in a magistrates' court appeals to the Crown Court.

reinstatement order an order made by an INDUSTRIAL TRIBUNAL that an employer must reinstate an employee who has been unfairly dismissed in his or her former job. The employee must be treated as if he or she had not been dismissed. *See also* RE-ENGAGEMENT ORDER.

reinsurance the procedure whereby an insurer insures itself with another insurer when the risk underwritten is too great for the insurer to bear alone.

rejection of goods a buyer's right to repudiate a contract of sale and reject goods when the vendor is in BREACH OF CONTRACT.

rejection of offer the refusal of an offer by the person to whom it is made. An offer is rejected if it is accepted subject to conditions or if the offeree makes a counter-offer. Once an offer has been rejected, it cannot be accepted later. *See* LAPSE OF OFFER; REVOCATION OF OFFER.

rejoinder the answer of a defendant to the reply of a plaintiff, which can only be served by leave of the court.

relation back the principle of referring an act back to a date before it actually took place, and from which it is considered to be effective. When PROBATE is granted, it relates back to the time of the testator's death.

relator a private individual at whose request or suggestion an action is commenced by the ATTORNEY GENERAL to enforce a public right or raise a matter of public interest.

release (1) the discharge of a person from custody (*see also* PAROLE). (2) renunciation of a claim against another person; a document by which a person discharges another from any claim.

relevance or **relevancy** in the law of EVIDENCE, a term that refers to a relationship between facts whereby one is probable because of the existence of the other. Unless excluded (e.g. HEARSAY EVIDENCE), all relevant facts are admissible.

relevant facts facts from which other facts in issue may be inferred.

relevant transfer the automatic transfer of a person's contract of employment from one company to another when a business changes ownership.

relief *see* REMEDY.

remainder an interest in land that comes into effect when a prior interest ends.

remand holding in custody or releasing on BAIL a person charged with a crime during an adjournment. The period is normally eight days; if it is to be longer, the accused must be released on bail unless there are special reasons not to do so.

remand centre a place where young offenders are detained while awaiting trial or sentence.

remedy, also called **redress** or **relief**, the means that the law provides for the recovery of a right or obtaining compensation for a wrong; the redress or relief that the court gives.

remission prior to 1991, the cancellation of part of a prisoner's SENTENCE, typically one third, for good behaviour.

remoteness of damage the degree to which a defendant is liable for the consequences of something he or she has done or has failed to do. In cases of BREACH OF CONTRACT, a defendant is only liable if damage done was reasonably likely.

removal of action the transfer of proceedings from one court to another, e.g. from the county court to the High Court.

rendition in INTERNATIONAL LAW, the doctrine that an offender can be returned to a state to be tried there, even if no EXTRADITION treaty is in existence.

renewal of lease the granting of a new LEASE on the same or similar terms as an earlier lease between the same parties.

renewal of writ the renewal of a WRIT for a further period of 12 months when the first 12-month period of validity has expired. It is usually permissible when, for example, a defendant has not been traced.

renouncing probate the refusal of an EXECUTOR to accept the role. *See* PROBATE.

rent periodic payments made by a TENANT to the owner of land for its occupation and use. The amount is stipulated in a LEASE or TENANCY agreement. If a tenant fails to pay, the landlord has a number of remedies open to him or her. *See* FAIR RENT.

rental period a period for which a TENANT or LESSEE must pay RENT. It is usually paid in arrears, unless agreed otherwise.

rent assessment committee a committee appointed by the Secretary of State to decide a dispute about what constitutes a FAIR RENT, or to consider the fairness of a proposed rent increase.

rentcharge a periodic payment for the use of land, other than the RENT stipulated by a LEASE or TENANCY agreement.

rent officer an officer appointed to keep a register of rents and to consider applications regarding FAIR RENTS.

rent tribunal a tribunal appointed by the Secretary of State for the Environment to consider matters arising in relation to rents under a RESTRICTED CONTRACT.

renunciation the intentional giving up of a right.

renvoi literally 'sending back'. In PRIVATE INTERNATIONAL LAW, the application by the courts of one country of the law of another country.

repatriation (1) sending a person back to his or her own country. (2) a person's voluntary resumption of his or her previous nationality.

repeal the abrogation of a STATUTE by a later statute. Any transaction completed before repeal is unaffected.

reply in PLEADINGS, a plaintiff's statement in answer to a defence or counterclaim; speech by COUNSEL for the plaintiff or for the prosecution answering the defence.

reporting restrictions limitations imposed by the court on the press and the broadcasting media in reporting proceedings.

repossession the exercising of a mortgagee's right to take possession of a mortgaged property, usually in cases where payments are in arrears.

representation (1) taking another person's place, e.g. as AGENT for a PRINCIPAL. (2) a statement made by one person to another that induces a course of action, e.g. the signing of a CONTRACT.

representative action an action brought by a number of persons who share an interest in the proceedings. Judgment is binding on all of them if their grievance is common and they can benefit from the relief claimed.

reprieve the formal suspending of the carrying out of a SENTENCE.

republication of will the re-execution, following the required formalities, of a WILL. The will can then be effective from the date of its republication and an alteration validated.

repudiation refusal to be bound by the terms of a CONTRACT. A person repudiating would usually be in BREACH OF CONTRACT.

repugnancy an inconsistency or contradiction in a DEED or other document. The court may strike out inconsistent or contradictory provisions that render ineffective the intentions of the parties to the document.

reputation the estimation in which a person is generally held. The damaging of a person's reputation may be DEFAMATION.

requisition (1) a demand by an intending purchaser of land for a search for encumbrances. (2) the compulsory taking of property.

resale *see* RIGHT OF RESALE.

resale price maintenance the imposition by a manufacturer of the minumum price at which something may be sold at retail. Generally, such a condition is void, with a small number of exceptions. One example, the Net Book Agreement, was recently abolished.

rescission a REMEDY in cases of BREACH OF CONTRACT, whereby an injured party may bring the contract to an end by performing no further part of it, recovering any part performed and seeking DAMAGES.

resealed probate the granting of PROBATE in one country, then approved in another, enabling an EXECUTOR to deal with the testator's property in the second country.

reservation (1) an action by a seller of land to retain a right over the land. (2) a limiting condition.

reservation of title *see* RETENTION OF TITLE.

reset in Scotland, knowingly possessing property that has been unlawfully acquired by another. *See* HANDLING.

res extincta literally 'non-existent thing'. There is no CONTRACT when an agreement is non-existent.

res gestae literally 'things done', used to refer to events that have happened and with which the court is concerned. Under the rule of RELEVANCE, such events are admissible as EVIDENCE.

residence the place where a person habitually lives; the place he or she calls home. A person's country of residence affects his or her tax liability.

residence order a court order stipulating with whom a child is to live.

residential occupier a person occupying premises as his or her residence and who enjoys the right to remain in occupation and restricts the right of any other person to recover possession.

residual negative principle in JURISPRUDENCE, the concept that anything that is not specifically prohibited by law is legally permitted.

residuary devise a gift of REAL PROPERTY made by WILL, as in 'all the rest of my property to . . .', i.e. after specific gifts have been satisfied.

residuary estate any part of a TESTATOR's property that is not specifically bequeathed.

residue what remains of a deceased person's ESTATE after payment of debts, funeral expenses, legacies, administration costs, etc.

resile to withdraw from something, such as an agreement.

res ipsa loquitur literally 'the thing speaks for itself'. In actions for NEGLIGENCE, the inference that the fact that an accident happened means that the defendant must have been negligent and there is a *PRIMA FACIE* case.

resisting arrest acting in such a way as to prevent oneself being arrested. It is an offence to resist legal arrest and may incur a charge of OBSTRUCTING A POLICE OFFICER.

res judicata literally 'a thing that has been decided'. It describes a final judicial decision made by a court of competent jurisdiction that may not be challenged. It does not preclude an APPEAL.

res nullius literally 'a thing that is nobody's'. In INTERNATIONAL LAW, it refers to territory that does not belong to any sovereign state.

resolution (1) a formal expression of opinion by a body, such as an assembly. (2) a decision made by the majority of members of a company.

respondeat superior literally 'let the principal answer'. The principle that an employer may be held responsible for certain wrongful acts committed by his or her employee in the course of employment.

respondent a person against whom a petition is presented or an appeal brought.

res sua literally 'his thing'. A CONTRACT is void if a person makes it to purchase something that he or she already owns.

restitutio in integrum literally 'restoration to the original position'. There is no right to rescind a CONTRACT (*see* RESCISSION) if it is impossible to restore things to how they were.

restitution restoring something to its rightful owner. A court may order a person convicted of possessing stolen goods to return them to the person lawfully entitled to own them.

restraint of marriage a condition in a CONTRACT that attempts to prevent someone from marrying. Such a condition is usually void as contrary to PUBLIC POLICY.

restraint of trade a clause in a CONTRACT that restricts a person's right to carry on his or her trade or business. Unless it can be shown not to be against PUBLIC POLICY, or has been entered into voluntarily, or is reasonable in the circumstances, such a condition is usually void.

restraints of princes in marine insurance, a phrase used to refer to political interference with a commercial undertaking by rulers or officials of other countries.

restricted contract prior to the Housing Act 1988, a contract for the right to occupy a dwelling in return for a RENT that included payment for the use of furniture and services.

restriction order a court order subjecting an offender to specific restrictions for a specified or unlimited time. *See* HOSPITAL ORDER.

restrictive covenant an obligation on an owner of land that restricts the uses to which the land may be put, often for the benefit of the owner of adjoining land. It is created by DEED.

restrictive endorsement a signature that prohibits further negotiation of a BILL OF EXCHANGE, e.g. by specifiying that it should be payable to one named person only.

restrictive trade practices certain types of agreement relating to the setting of prices, terms of supply, etc, which are considered to be against the public interest unless registered with the Director General of Fair Trading. *See* RESALE PRICE MAINTENANCE.

resulting trust a TRUST created when beneficial interest is returned to the settlor by virtue of being incompletely disposed of.

retention of title or **reservation of title** in contracts of sale, the stipulation that the ownership of goods remains with the vendor until full payment has been received. It is sometimes referred to as a 'Romalpa clause' from a 1976 action.

retirement of jury the time during which a JURY considers its VERDICT. It follows the SUMMING UP and no further EVIDENCE can be called.

retortion or **retorsion** in INTERNATIONAL LAW, retaliation by a state against an objectionable act by another state. Examples include revoking diplomatic privileges.

retour sans protêt literally 'return without protest'. A request or direction that a dishonoured BILL OF EXCHANGE should be returned without protest.

retrospective legislation or **retroactive legislation** laws that affect acts carried out before they were passed. It is generally presumed that statutes are not intended to apply retroactively.

return (1) the results of votes cast and counted in an election. (2) a document containing a company's formal report.

returning officer a person appointed to be responsible for the proper conducting of parliamentary elections.

revenue statutes Acts of Parliament concerned with matters relating to taxation.

reversal of judgment the altering of all or part of a judgment on APPEAL.

reversion or **revertor** an interest in land where a person has granted an interest lesser than his own and retains the rest of his or her interest. If the first person grants an interest for the lifetime of a second person, the latter's interest reverts to the former on death.

reversionary lease a LEASE that is to be effective at some future date. Such leases are void unless thay take effect within 21 years of being granted.

revival of will the reviving by re-execution of a WILL that has been revoked. The will then takes effect from the date of revival.

revocation the annulment of something already done.

revocation of offer the withdrawal by the offerer of an offer. An offer can be revoked before acceptance provided the offeree is made aware and there is no OPTION in force.

revocation of patent the revoking by the court of a PATENT on a number of grounds, such as that the invention was not patentable, that the patent was granted to a person not entitled to it, etc.

revocation of probate cancellation by the court of a grant of PROBATE on the grounds that an EXECUTOR is incapacitated and cannot act, or because probate was obtained by FRAUD.

revocation of will action by a TESTATOR to revoke a WILL. It can be done at any time before the death of the testator and may be effected by destruction of the will, the writing of a new will, or the addition of a CODICIL.

right (1) something to which a person has just and lawful claim. (2) a title to or interest in property. *See* HUMAN RIGHTS; NATURAL RIGHTS.

right of abode the RIGHT, which may be granted by the Secretary of State, to live permanently in the UK.

right of action the RIGHT to bring an action in court.

right of audience the RIGHT of an ADVOCATE to be heard during court proceedings.

right of entry the RIGHT to repossess land by entering it. The right may be exercised if a LESSEE is in BREACH OF CONTRACT.

right of light *see* EASEMENT OF LIGHT.

right of resale the RIGHT of a seller of goods to resell the goods if his or her purchaser fails to pay the agreed price.

right of silence the RIGHT of a person charged with an offence or being tried for a crime not to answer questions or give EVIDENCE. It is intended to protect the innocent, but may work against a defendant's interests if inferences are drawn from his or her refusal to answer.

right of support the RIGHT to have one's building supported by an adjoining building or the soil of one's land supported by the soil on adjoining land.

right of way the RIGHT to pass over another person's land. A public right of way is enjoyed by the public at large and may be created by STATUTE.

rights issue raising share capital from a company's existing shareholders by offering further SHARES, usually in proportion to existing holdings.

right to begin the RIGHT of a party to an action to open the action. The right is usually conferred on the party who bears the BURDEN OF PROOF. In criminal cases, the prosecution has the right to begin.

riot the use or threat of unlawful violence by a gathering of 12 or more persons whose conduct causes a reasonable person to fear for his or her personal safety.

riparian relating to the bank of a stream or river.

road a HIGHWAY or other type of route to which the public has access. In cases of road traffic offences, it is important to define a 'road' clearly. Generally, it must be a route from one place to another but includes bridges and privately owned roads.

robbery the offence of stealing accompanied by the use or threat of force against a person.

rolled-up plea a defence of FAIR COMMENT used in actions for LIBEL, that the words used are statements of fact, and opinions expressed constitute fair comment.

Romalpa clause *see* RETENTION OF TITLE.

room standard the number of rooms in a dwelling house deemed necessary to accommodate the number of people living in it.

root of title a document that describes land to be sold and identifies the whole legal and equitable interest. It must also cast no doubt on the title.

royal assent a formality that makes a Bill into an ACT OF PARLIAMENT.

royal prerogative the constitutional power that the Crown may exercise. Most acts are done by the government; some are done by the Sovereign on the advice of the government.

royalty an amount payable to the owner of a property (such as the author of a book) in return for the use of that property (by the publisher).

rules of court rules, made by a body authorized to make them, governing the practice and procedure of a court.

Rules of the Supreme Court (RSC) the rules governing the practice and procedure of the SUPREME COURT.

S

sabotage malicious damage to or destruction of property, e.g. of the state for political reasons, or of an employer during an industrial dispute. A charge of CRIMINAL DAMAGE may be brought.

sacrilege the offence of breaking into and committing an offence in a place of worship.

safety at work the duty placed on an employer to safeguard the health and safety at work of his or her employees.

sale a CONTRACT for the sale of goods or the transfer of land.
sale by description a CONTRACT for the sale of goods that contains a description of the goods, which must match their description.
sale by the court a sale of property by order of the court, e.g. to enforce a MORTGAGE.
sale of goods a CONTRACT under the terms of which the seller agrees to transfer the ownership of goods to a buyer in exchange for an agreed price.
sale or return, also known as **sale on approval**, the delivery of goods to a person who can then keep them for a specified time before deciding whether or not to buy them.
salvage the reward offered to a person who saves a ship or other maritime property from shipwreck or other fate. If no salvage agreement exists, the salvor may be entitled to such a reward, which will be assessed by the court.
sanction (1) a measure taken to punish a crime. (2) a solemn agreement. (3) action taken against a state that is in breach of INTERNATIONAL LAW.
sanity *see* PRESUMPTION OF SANITY.
sans recours literally 'without recourse [to me]', words used on a BILL OF EXCHANGE to indicate that an endorser is not liable.
satisfaction (1) the fulfilling of a claim. (2) the doctrine that payment, performance or some other act discharges an obligation.
satisfied term a TERM OF YEARS created for a purpose now fulfilled.
scandalous statement an abusive or irrelevant statement that, if it appears in PLEADINGS or an AFFIDAVIT, may be struck out.
schedule (1) a formal list. (2) an appendix to an ACT OF PARLIAMENT listing supplementary details.
scheme of arrangement an agreement between a debtor and creditors for the payment of debts to avoid the BANKRUPTCY of the debtor.

***scienter* rule** a rule governing an owner's liability for the behaviour of his or her animal. Any animal that may cause damage must be kept secured.
scuttling deliberately sinking a ship in order to make an insurance claim.
seal wax impressed and attached to a document to authenticate it.
search *see* POWER OF SEARCH.
searches examinations made of the registers of land to find if any encumbrances exist.
search warrant a WARRANT issued by a magistrate or a High Court judge authorizing the entry to and searching of premises for stolen goods, firearms, proscribed drugs, etc.
seaworthiness the condition of a ship and its crew when it is fit for the voyage and to carry its cargo safely.
secondary evidence a form of EVIDENCE that suggests that better evidence is available. *See* PRIMARY EVIDENCE.
secondary party *see* PRINCIPAL.
secondary picketing *see* PICKETING.
Secretary of State a member of the government in charge of a government department.
secret profits profits made by an AGENT without the knowledge of his or her PRINCIPAL.
secret trust a TRUST, the existence and terms of which are unknown, whereby a TESTATOR gives property to a person on that person's promise to hold it in trust for a third party.
section 8 orders in family proceedings, court orders that settle details of the care and upbringing of children. A *residence order* settles where a child is to live; a *contact order* deals with the contact the child is to have with other people; a *prohibited steps order* stipulates what steps may not be taken without the court's permission.
secure accommodation accommodation in which children in care and with a history of absconding are placed.

secured creditor a person who holds a security, such as a mortgage, for money lent.

secure tenancy prior to 1988, the TENANCY on a dwelling where the LANDLORD was a local authority or housing association and the TENANT occupied the dwelling as his or her principal or only home. The tenancy could only be terminated if the landlord obtained a possession order in the court.

securities things that are lodged to ensure the fulfilling of an obligation: STOCKS, SHARES, DEBENTURES, and other rights to receive dividends and interest.

security of tenure the right of a TENANT to occupy premises and statutory protection restricting a LANDLORD's right to gain possession.

sedition the speaking or writing of words intended to bring into contempt, or incite disaffection against, the Sovereign, the government and the administration of justice of the UK, or to promote feelings of hostility among different classes of British subjects.

seditious libel SEDITION in the form of written words.

seduction (1) persuading a person to have illicit sexual intercourse. (2) enticing a person to disobedience or desertion, e.g. seducing a member of HM Forces from allegiance to the Crown.

seisin the feudal possession of freehold land, now synonymous with POSSESSION.

select committee a committee appointed by either or both Houses of Parliament to investigate and report on matters of interest to them.

self-defence the use of reasonable force to defend oneself or one's property against attack or the threat of attack. It may be a DEFENCE in cases of HOMICIDE.

self-employed a term describing a person in gainful employment who is not an employee. Statutory rights and protections do not apply to the self-employed.

self-help action taken by a person to protect his or her rights without resorting to the courts. Such action may be permitted in, for example, cases of TRESPASS.

self-incrimination giving answers to questions, or evidence, that might lead to oneself being prosecuted. *See* RIGHT OF SILENCE.

seller a person who sells or agrees to sell goods or land (more usually referred to as the *vendor*).

sentence the punishment imposed by the court on a person who pleads guilty to an offence or who has been found guilty by a JURY. It is usually within the court's discretion to recommend an appropriate sentence. *See* MAXIMUM SENTENCE; MINIMUM SENTENCE; MITIGATION.

separate trials *see* JOINDER OF OFFENDERS.

separation agreement an agreement between husband and wife, following the breakdown of their marriage, that releases each from the duty of COHABITATION. For such agreement to be valid, they have to show that the marriage has already broken down. Separation may be grounds for DIVORCE if the partners have lived apart for two years and neither contests the petition; or for five years, when consent is not required.

separation of powers the division into separate, independent institutions of the legislative, executive and judicial functions of government, designed to safeguard individual liberty.

sequestration (1) a WRIT authorizing the entering and seizing of a person's estate where that person has failed to obey an INJUNCTION. (2) in Scotland, the terms used for BANKRUPTCY.

Serious Fraud Office a body established in 1987 to investigate and prosecute cases of complex and serious FRAUD. It is headed by a Director appointed by the ATTORNEY GENERAL.

service delivery of a SUMMONS or WRIT, in person or by post.

service law the body of law that regulates the conduct of members of the armed forces: naval law, military law and air-force law.

servient tenement land over which there is an encumbrance, such as an EASEMENT.

set-off a plea that counterbalances a claim and should therefore extinguish it, as when a debtor shows that a creditor owes him or her money.

setting aside a court order that cancels or makes void another order or judgment.

settled land land that is subject to a SETTLEMENT, in which two or more beneficial interests exist in succession, e.g. land held in trust.

settlement a disposition of land made by DEED or WILL. Trusts are created and designate the beneficiaries and the terms under which they are to take the property.

settlement of action the voluntary coming to terms by parties to an action and the discontinuance of the action. Such settlement may be reached at any time.

settlor a person who makes a SETTLEMENT in regard to property.

severalty possession of property by several persons, separately and exclusively.

sex discrimination acting to the disadvantage of a person because of his or her gender, in matters relating to remuneration, supply of goods and services, etc. There are several statutory offences under the Equal Pay and Sex Discrimination Acts.

shadow director a person actually involved in the running of a business, but ostensibly not a director, therefore free from a director's liabilities and duties.

sham marriage a lawful marriage, but one that is designed to avoid immigration regulations, etc.

share capital the total amount that the shareholders in a company have contributed in the form of payment for their shares.

shares interests in an incorporated company measured by a sum of money. Share-holding confers voting rights and a right to share profits (in the form of dividends). *Preference shares* rank above *ordinary shares* (which constitute the risk capital). *Redeemable shares* can be bought back by the company.

shareholder a person who owns SHARES in a company.

sheriff the chief officer of the Crown in a county, responsible for the administering of justice and conducting parliamentary elections.

shoplifting stealing goods from a shop, i.e. MAKING OFF WITHOUT PAYMENT.

short cause list a list of cases to be heard in the High Court, without a JURY and expected to last less than four hours.

silk *see* QUEEN'S COUNSEL.

similar-fact evidence evidence offered that an accused has previously acted in the way with which he or she is presently charged. Such evidence is only admissible if deemed relevant.

simple contract a CONTRACT, which may be written or oral, and not made by DEED. It is also called a 'parol contract'.

simple trust *see* BARE TRUST.

sine die literally 'without a day', indefinitely.

sittings four periods in the year when the SUPREME COURT sits. They are Michaelmas, Hilary, Easter and Trinity.

slander spoken words that constitute DEFAMATION. *See also* LIBEL.

slander of goods making false and malicious statements disparaging goods, the tort of MALICIOUS FALSEHOOD. The words used must assert that the goods are defective.

slander of title a form of MALICIOUS FALSEHOOD when false and malicious statements are made regarding the plaintiff's right to sell property.

slip rule the rule by which the court may correct a clerical error in an order or judgment, or errors arising from an accidental slip or omission.

small claims claims, most commonly made by consumers against commercial businesses, for small amounts. Cases are referred to arbitration in the county courts.

smuggling the unlawful importing or exporting of goods without payment of the duty levied on them.

social inquiry report a report submitted to the court, usually by a PROBATION OFFICER, to assist it in deciding what SENTENCE to impose on a convicted person. The report gives details of family background, home circumstances, employment prospects, etc.

soliciting (1) the offence of attempting to obtain clients for the purposes of PROSTITUTION in a street or other public place. (2) the persistent accosting of a woman in a public place for the purposes of prostitution, also known as KERB CRAWLING.

solicitor a person qualified to conduct legal proceedings and to give advice on legal matters. Solicitors must have passed examinations set by the Law Society, and have been awarded a certificate authorizing them to practise.

Solicitor-General a LAW OFFICER OF THE CROWN, subordinate to the ATTORNEY GENERAL. The Solicitor-General is usually a member of the government.

Solicitors' Disciplinary Tribunal a committee appointed by the MASTER OF THE ROLLS to hear complaints made against solicitors. The Tribunal's powers extend to striking off a SOLICITOR against whom a complaint is upheld.

solicitor's lien the method a SOLICITOR may use to protect his or her rights to recover costs from a client. A *retaining lien* allows the solicitor to keep papers, chattels, etc, belonging to the client until payment is made; alternatively, the solicitor may have a lien on personal property of the client.

solitary confinement a form of IMPRISONMENT where a prisoner is not allowed contact with any other prisoner.

solvent abuse the inhaling of fumes from glue or other solvents to induce intoxication. It is an offence to supply such a substance to anyone under the age of 18 if the supplier knows or believes it will be abused.

space standard *see* ROOM STANDARD.

special business resolutions, etc, made at a company's extraordinary general meeting. It is distinct from general business transacted at an annual general meeting.

special case in civil actions, a statement of facts agreed between the parties and submitted to the court for an opinion on points of law.

special damages in a claim for DAMAGES, those that would not be presumed, such as loss of earnings and medical expenses.

special defence a DEFENCE confined to individual offences and peculiar to one type of action. Examples include FAIR COMMENT in an action for DEFAMATION.

special hospital an institution that holds dangerous and violent offenders, and those requiring special degrees of security.

special jury until 1971, a JURY composed only of persons who owned property above a specific rateable value.

special manager a person appointed by the court to prepare accounts and perform other duties for a company that has gone into liquidation.

special plea a PLEA IN BAR. *See AUTREFOIS ACQUIT*, *AUTREFOIS CONVICT*.

special resolution a resolution passed by a majority of not less than 75 per cent of those entitled to vote.

special verdict a VERDICT of not guilty of the grounds of INSANITY.

specification in a PATENT application, information about an invention's construction, mode of operation, etc.

specific goods goods identified exactly in a contract for the sale of goods. Articles not so identified are called *unascertained goods*.

specific issue order *see* SECTION 8 ORDERS.

specific performance a court order that an individual must fulfil the terms of a CONTRACT to which he or she is a party.

specimen a sample of blood, breath or urine taken from a person suspected of the offence of driving with more than the permitted level of alcohol.

speeding offence driving a motor vehicle at more than the permitted speed. In certain circumstances, emergency vehicles may be exempt from speed restrictions.

spent conviction a previous conviction that need not be disclosed following a REHABILITATION PERIOD.

split trial a trial in which liability and an award of DAMAGES are heard separately.

spying or **espionage** obtaining information that may be used by an individual or government hostile to the state. *See* OFFICIAL SECRETS.

squatter a person wrongfully occupying land. *See* TRESPASS.

stag a person who acquires shares in a company with the intention of selling them to make a profit.

stamp duty a tax imposed on certain legal documents.

standard of proof the degree of proof required to win a civil case or secure a conviction in a criminal case. *See* BURDEN OF PROOF; PROOF BEYOND REASONABLE DOUBT.

standing mute remaining mute when asked to plead. If deliberately silent (called *mute of malice*) an accused will have a plea of NOT GUILTY entered; a deaf and dumb person is considered to be mute 'by visitation of God'.

stare decisis literally 'to stand by things decided', the concept that underlies the doctrine of PRECEDENT.

stateless person an individual who has no NATIONALITY.

statement of affairs in cases of BANKRUPTCY, a statement that details creditors, debts, liabilities, assets, etc.

statement of claim a statement by a PLAINTIFF that gives details of the facts on which his or her case relies and what relief is sought.

statement of defence a statement by a DEFENDANT in civil cases dealing with the allegations of the PLAINTIFF in his or her STATEMENT OF CLAIM.

status a person's legal standing, as belonging to a group in society to which particular rights and duties are ascribed.

statute an ACT OF PARLIAMENT, the 'highest form of law'.

statute book the body of existing ACTS OF PARLIAMENT.

statutory declaration a declaration made before a person authorized to administer an OATH but not made in court.

stay of execution the suspending of the carrying out of a judgment or court order.

stay of proceedings a court order that suspends proceedings, usually enforced because of misconduct by the PLAINTIFF.

stipendiary magistrate a full-time MAGISTRATE who usually sits alone and usually has the power of two lay magistrates.

stop and search powers a power of the police to stop and search persons or vehicles in a public place, or a place to which the public has access, for stolen goods, offensive weapons, etc.

street offences unlawful acts that are related to the use of streets, e.g. OBSTRUCTION.

strict liability in criminal cases, liability where, exceptionally, *MENS REA* does not have to be present.

strict settlement the conferring by TRUST of beneficial interests in land with the intention of keeping the land in the settlor's family.

striking off the removal from a register of a professionally qualified person for PROFESSIONAL MISCONDUCT.

structured settlement in cases of serious personal injury, a settlement whereby the injured party receives, in addition to a lump sum, periodic payments to cover future need.

subject to contract the phrase used to prevent a document being taken to represent a concluded bargain.

sub judice under judicial consideration, not yet decided. The *sub judice* rule makes it an offence of CONTEMPT OF COURT to publish comments that might prejudice a fair trial.

sub-lease a LEASE shorter than another lease and granted by a person who is already a LESSEE, also known as a *subtenancy* or *underlease*.

sub-mortgage the borrowing by a MORTGAGEE on the security of an existing MORTGAGE.

subornation the procuring of another person to commit an offence. It applies particularly to PERJURY.

subpoena an order to a person to appear on a certain date in court to give EVIDENCE. A person who fails to obey a subpoena is in CONTEMPT OF COURT.

subrogation substituting one person for another, as when an insurer exercises a right to enforce a claim that the insured could have claimed against a third party.

sub rosa literally 'under the rose', confidential.

subscribing witness a person who signs a document as an attesting WITNESS.

subsequent pleadings in civil actions, PLEADINGS made after the plaintiff's REPLY, which can only be served with leave of the court.

substantial damages an award of DAMAGES given when actual damage has been caused to the plaintiff.

substantive law the part of the law that is concerned with rights, duties, liabilities, etc. *See* ADJECTIVE LAW.

substituted service in civil litigation, the SERVICE of documents when it is not possible in person or by post. Leave of the court is required and substituted service may take the form of advertisement.

substitutional legacy a LEGACY that passes gifts to the descendants of a BENEFICIARY where the beneficiary predeceases the TESTATOR.

subtenancy *see* SUB-LEASE.

sue to make a claim for a REMEDY through proceedings in the civil courts.

suicide the killing of oneself intentionally and voluntarily. It is not itself a crime but there are a number of statutory offences associated with it, including aiding or abetting a suicide.

sui juris literally 'of his own right', the term used to describe a person who has full legal capacity.

suit (1) a claim in court. (2) also used of LITIGATION in general.

summary conviction a CONVICTION in a magistrates' court. The magistrates judge both fact and law.

summary offences offences, mostly minor, that are tried by a magistrate and without a JURY.

summary trial a trial by magistrates and without a JURY.

summing up the judge's final speech before a JURY retires to consider its VERDICT. The judge summarizes the case and directs the jury on points of law.

summons in both civil and criminal cases, a court order to a person to appear in court at a specified place on a specified date.

superior court a court whose JURISDICTION is not limited by geographical area or category of actions. The House of Lords, the Court of Appeal and the High Court are all superior courts. *See also* INFERIOR COURT.

supervision order a court order that places a child under the supervision of a local authority or a PROBATION OFFICER.

suppression of documents the offence of destroying, defacing or concealing documents filed in a court or a government department for personal gain.

Supreme Court the Court of Appeal, the High Court of Justice and the Crown Court. Its practice and proceedure are regulated by the RULES OF THE SUPREME COURT.

surety (1) a person who gives security for someone else. *See* BAIL. (2) a sum of money deposited and forfeited if a person fails to appear in court.

surprise in court procedure, an event that may give grounds for a new trial because it has placed a litigant at a disadvantage.

surrender of tenancy the giving up by a TENANT to a LANDLORD of a LEASE. The surrender may be *express* and usually in the form of a DEED; *implied surrender* occurs when both parties act in such a way as to indicate that the lease is terminated.

surrender to custody to give oneself into the custody of the police or the court. It is necessary to surrender to custody to obtain release on BAIL.

sus law the law, abolished in 1981, that gave the police powers to arrest a person suspected of loitering with the intention of committing an arrestable offence.

suspended sentence a SENTENCE that the court orders should not take place immediately. A sentence of more than two years cannot be suspended.

T

tail *see* ENTAILED INTEREST.

tail general an ENTAILED INTEREST in which descendants who can succeed to land are any issue of the tenant in tail.

tail male general an ENTAILED INTEREST in which only male descendants of the tenant in tail may succeed.

tail special an ENTAILED INTEREST in which only the descendants of the tenant in tail and one specified spouse may succeed.

tangible property *see* PROPERTY.

taxation of costs an examination by an officer of the court of the lawyers' bills of costs, to ensure that the sums are fair in view of the work to be done. *See* TAXING MASTER.

tax avoidance the lawful arranging of one's affairs to reduce one's liability for tax.

tax evasion the unlawful act of frustrating assessment for tax by concealing income, etc.

taxing master an official of the SUPREME COURT appointed to carry out TAXATION OF COSTS.

telephone tapping secretly monitoring telephone conversations by interfering with the line. It is a form of ELECTRONIC SURVEILLANCE and is illegal unless authorized by the Home Secretary.

tenancy the relationship of a TENANT to the land that he or she holds but that belongs to another.

tenant an individual or a company granted a LEASE.

tenant for life a person who owns land for the whole of his or her own life. The equitable interest terminates on the tenant's death.

tender (1) an offer to purchase or supply goods or services. (2) to offer money or other form of payment to discharge a debt or an obligation.

tender before action a DEFENDANT's plea that he or she had offered to satisfy the PLAINTIFF's claim before a WRIT was issued. The plea is supported by payment into court of the relevant sum.

tenement property held by TENURE.

tenure the relationship between landlord and tenant that determined the terms on which land was held. The feudal forms of tenure were mostly abolished in the 1920s. *See* FREEHOLD.

term of years or **term for years** an interest in land that subsists for a specified length of time.

term of years absolute a TERM OF YEARS that may or may not be brought to an end by forfeiture or notice, but not by the death of any person.

territorial waters the sea area adjacent to a state's shoreline and within its exclusive JURISDICTION.

terrorism the use of violence for political ends and to put the public in fear. *See* HIJACKING; PROSCRIBED ORGANIZATION.

testament a WILL that disposes of a person's personal property but not land; usually refers to a will without that distinction.

testamentary freedom a person's right to dispose of his or her property as he or she wishes. There are statutes that limit this freedom, such as the Inheritance Act 1975.

testate on death, having left a valid WILL. *See* INTESTACY.

testator a deceased person who has made a WILL.

test case an action that determines the legal position of people who are not party to the action.

testimonial evidence assertions offered as proof of what is being asserted. It includes that which the WITNESS perceived with his or her own senses and HEARSAY EVIDENCE.

testimony a statement in court by a WITNESS, usually on OATH, offered as EVIDENCE of what is being asserted.

theft the dishonest appropriation of property that belongs to someone else with the intention of depriving the rightful owner of it permanently.

thing in action *see* CHOSE IN ACTION.

third party any person other than the principals in proceedings, or other than the parties to a CONTRACT.

third-party insurance INSURANCE against risk to any person other than the parties to the policy.

third-party proceedings proceedings brought separately for a REMEDY from a person who is not already a party to the action.

threatening behaviour the offence of threatening to use unlawful violence against a person or persons. It is also an offence to use insulting words and behaviour such that the person against whom they are used believes there exists a real threat of physical violence.

tied cottage a dwelling provided for a TENANT who has a service tenancy, most commonly an agricultural worker.

tied house a PUBLIC HOUSE of which the LESSEE has covenanted to purchase all of his or her supplies of beers, etc, from the LESSOR (most commonly a brewery).

title (1) a person's right of ownership of property, or evidence of that right. (2) the heading of an ACT OF PARLIAMENT.

title deeds documents that show evidence of the rightful ownership of land.

tort any wrongful act or omission for which DAMAGES may be claimed in a civil action, other than BREACH OF CONTRACT. The word '*tort*' is Old French for 'wrong' or 'harm'.

tortfeasor a person who commits a TORT. *See also* JOINT TORTFEASORS.

torture the offence, while acting in an official capacity, of inflicting severe pain or suffering on another person in the performance of official duties.

totting up the system of accumulating penalty points for motoring and road traffic offences. When enough points have been awarded against a licence holder, he or she may be disqualified from driving.

tracing trust property the process used by beneficiaries to recover trust property that has come into the hands of others.

trade description a direct or indirect description of goods for sale. Under the Trade Descriptions Act 1968, it is an offence to describe goods falsely.

trade dispute a dispute between an employer and his or her employees on matters such as rates of pay, working conditions, etc.

trade mark a symbol that identifies a manufacturer's products and is intended to be recognized by the public. It may consist of a design, a word or a name and, if registered, enjoys certain protections.

trade secret a process or product that is part of a company's business. the disclosure of which to a competitor would harm the owner's business. Injunctions can be obtained to prevent the disclosure of trade secrets.

transfer the conveyancing of ownership of land from one person to another, usually by DEED.

transfer of risk the passing of the potential for loss from the seller to the buyer. Goods remain at the seller's risk until ownership transfers to the buyer.

traverse the denial of an allegation made in a STATEMENT OF CLAIM.

treason a breach of allegiance to the Crown, first defined in 1351. Modern forms of treason include waging war against the sovereign and giving aid and comfort to the sovereign's enemies in times of war.

treasure trove valuable items, hidden by an untraceable owner, which belong to the Crown, not to the person who found them. It refers mostly to hidden gold and silver.

Treasury Solicitor an official who advises the Treasury on legal matters, instructs parliamentary counsel on Bills and acts as QUEEN'S PROCTOR.

treaty a written and signed agreement between states and governed by INTERNATIONAL LAW.

trespass an unlawful interference with a person or with a person's possession of land or goods. It is an actionable TORT and it is not necessary to show that actual damage has been caused.

trespass *ab initio* literally 'trespass from the beginning'. An offence of TRESPASS committed by a person who is authorized to enter another's land but then commits an unlawful act.

trial a formal investigation and determination of matters between parties in court. Most trials are conducted in public (but *see* IN CAMERA). *See also* SUMMARY TRIAL.

trial on indictment a TRIAL by JURY in the Crown Court of a person charged with an INDICTABLE OFFENCE.

tribunal a body with administrative or judicial powers but outside the court system. Tribunals are usually made up of lawyers and lay people with specialist knowledge and experience. They are convened to hear and judge, for example, industrial disputes.

trust an arrangement that imposes on a TRUSTEE an obligation to perform specific duties in relation to the holding and controlling of property on behalf of and for the benefit of others, known as beneficiaries.

trust documents documents held by TRUSTEES containing information in which beneficiaries have an interest and which they are entitled to know.

trustee a person who holds and controls property in TRUST for someone else (the BENEFICIARY).

trustee in bankruptcy in cases of BANKRUPTCY, the bankrupt's property is vested in a TRUSTEE who must collect the bankrupt's assets, sell them and distribute the proceeds among the bankrupt's creditors.

trust for sale a TRUST under which TRUSTEES must sell the trust property and hold the proceeds for the beneficiaries.

trust instrument the document that creates a SETTLEMENT and appoints TRUSTEES.

turning Queen's evidence *see* QUEEN'S EVIDENCE.

U

uberrimae fidei literally 'of the utmost good faith'. In the making of a CONTRACT, the principle that the promisee must inform the promiser of all the facts and circumstances that might influence his or her decision as to whether or not to enter into the contract.

ultra vires literally 'beyond the powers', a term describing the exceeding of legal powers and authority, especially by a corporation, of those conferred on it.

unascertained goods *see* SPECIFIC GOODS.

undefended cause a cause in which the DEFENDANT does not acknowledge service of the WRIT, fails to give notice of his or her intention to defend, and does not appear in court.

underlease *see* SUB-LEASE.

under protest acknowledging the service of a WRIT but denying an obligation to appear in the case.

undischarged bankrupt a person who has not been discharged from BANKRUPTCY and is therefore disqualified from holding certain offices, including Member of Parliament and JUSTICE OF THE PEACE.

undue influence pressure that prevents a person from exercising proper judgment in relation to a transaction. A CONTRACT entered into under undue influence may be set aside by the court.

unenforceable contract a valid CONTRACT but one that cannot be enforced because of a defect, such as a lapse of time.

unfair dismissal the termination of a person's employment for reasons that are judged unfair by an INDUSTRIAL TRIBUNAL. *See* RE-ENGAGEMENT ORDER; REINSTATEMENT ORDER.

unfavourable witness a WITNESS who is called to prove a fact but who fails to prove it or proves an opposite fact.

unfit to plead a term that describes a person's inability to PLEAD due to mental incapacity. Evidence of unfitness is required from two medical practitioners.

unilateral contract a CONTRACT where the promiser offers to pay in return for the performance of an act, and the promisee performs the act and is taken to have assented.

unity of seisin the ownership by the same person of two plots of land.

unlawful assembly *see* VIOLENT DISORDER.

unlawful wounding the offence of maliciously and unlawfully wounding a person with the intention of inflicting GRIEVOUS BODILY HARM. PROVOCATION is not a defence.

unliquidated damages an award of DAMAGES the level of which is not predetermined but depends on the circumstances of the particular case.

unopposed proceedings PROCEEDINGS in which a person entitled to oppose has not taken the opportunity offered to do so.

unpaid seller a person who has sold goods but has not received full payment for them, or has received a cheque or other form of payment that has been dishonoured. The seller has certain rights over the goods even though ownership has passed to the purchaser.

unreasonable conduct in matrimonial legislation, conduct such that the petitioner could not reasonably be expected to live with the respondent. Such conduct includes physical violence and persistent drunkenness.

unsolicited goods goods sent or delivered unrequested. Ownership transfers to the recipient unless the sender takes back the goods within six months or at the recipient's request. It is an offence to demand payment for unsolicited goods.

unsworn evidence EVIDENCE not given on OATH or by affirmation *(see* AFFIRM). A child's evidence is unsworn.

urine test the testing of a sample of urine for alcohol, illicit drugs, etc. *See* SPECIMEN.

use and occupation a claim based on a person's use and occupation of another's land but in the absence of a LEASE.

utmost good faith *see UBERRIMAE FIDEI.*

utter Bar *see* OUTER BAR.

V

vacant possession a term describing premises sold or offered for sale and not subject to a LEASE. If there is no agreement to the contrary, the vendor must give vacant possession on COMPLETION.

vacations periods between SITTINGS of the SUPREME COURT. They are Long, Christmas, Easter and Whitsun Vacations.

vagrant one of several groups defined in 1824 as 'idle and disorderly persons', 'rogues and vagabonds' or 'incorrigible rogues'. They include illegal pedlars, prostitutes, tramps and beggars.

vandalism the defacing or destroying of property. It is not an offence but a perpetrator may be charged with CRIMINAL DAMAGE.

variance a difference between a statement in a WRIT and in PLEADINGS, or between pleadings and EVIDENCE.

vendor a person who sells something, most commonly used of a seller of land.

venire de novo literally 'to come anew', a WRIT that annuls a trial and orders a new trial.

verdict the decision of a JURY as to the guilt or innocence of an accused, and considered in secret after all the evidence has been heard and the judge has summed-up. *See* NOT PROVEN.

vest to confer legal ownership or rights upon someone.

vexatious action a frivolous action or one brought to annoy an opponent, which may be struck out by the court. A person who brings such actions is referred to as a *vexatious litigant.*

vicarious performance the performance of all or part of a CONTRACT by someone who is not a party to it. The obligation does not transfer.

view the inspection by a judge of a place or thing outside the court, which constitutes a fact in issue.

vindictive damages *see* EXEMPLARY DAMAGES.

violent disorder the offence when three or more persons use or threaten to use unlawful physical violence sufficient to cause a reasonable person to fear for his or her personal safety. It replaced the common law offence of *unlawful assembly.*

visa an endorsement on a passport that indicates that it has been inspected and found correct. In certain cases it is made to allow entry into a foreign country by that country's authorities.

visitor a person appointed to inspect and report on institutions, and to inquire into irregularities.

void without force, having no legal effect.

voir dire literally 'to speak the truth'. (1) the phrase used of the preliminary examination of a WITNESS or JUROR to determine competence. (2) an inquiry by a judge into the admissibility of some evidence, such as a CONFESSION.

volenti non fit injuria literally 'no wrong is done to him who consents'. A defence that the plaintiff consented to an act, which cannot therefore be considered an injury.

voluntary liquidation *see* VOLUNTARY WINDING-UP.

voluntary winding-up or **voluntary liquidation** the WINDING-UP of a company so that the company and its creditors may settle their affairs before coming to court.

W

waiver abandonment or non-assertion of a legal right.

waiver of tort the relinquishing of the right to SUE for a TORT in favour of some other REMEDY.

war crimes criminal acts that violate the laws and customs of war. The term was used to describe murder, manslaughter and culpable homicide committed between September 1939 and June 1945 in Germany or places under German occupation. It is now applied more generally, e.g. to acts committed in former Yugoslavia in the 1990s.

ward a person who is under the protection and care of another person or the court.

warning of *caveat* a notice served on someone who has entered a *caveat* to appear and declare his or her interest.

warrant (1) a document authorizing action. (2) a document issued by a MAGISTRATE ordering that someone be arrested and brought before the court. *See also* SEARCH WARRANT.

warranty in CONTRACT law, a term or promise that, if breached, entitles the innocent party to DAMAGES. The term is used colloquially to describe a manufacturer's promise to repair or replace defective goods.

waste acts or omissions by a TENANT that adversely affect land or buildings. *See* PERMISSIVE WASTE.

wasting assets property that has a declining value, such as leaseholds.

wasting police time the offence of knowingly causing police manpower and resources to be wastefully used. It includes making false reports.

weekly tenancy a TENANCY from week to week.

White Book, The *see* RULES OF THE SUPREME COURT.

wilful misconduct wrongful behaviour by a person who knows it to be wrong and disregards the consequences of it.

wilful refusal to consummate a decision not to consummate a marriage on grounds that cannot be justified.

will a declaration of the intentions of a person regarding the disposal of his or her property on death. A will must be in writing and be signed and witnessed by two or more witnesses. A person making a will is called a TESTATOR. *See also* CODICIL; EXECUTOR; PRIVILEGED WILL; TESTAMENT.

winding up the termination of a company when it is insolvent. The winding up may be compulsory or voluntary.

with costs a term that describes a successful party's entitlement to claim COSTS from the other party.

withdrawal of issue from jury a procedure by which a judge discharges a JURY and finds for the opponent, or directs the jury to find in the opponent's favour, when he or she considers there is insufficient evidence to support a plaintiff's contention.

without prejudice *see* PREJUDICE.

without recourse [to me] *see SANS RECOURS.*

witness (1) a person who gives formal or sworn EVIDENCE at a hearing. (2) to give evidence or PROOF.

wounding inflicting an injury that breaks the skin.

wounding with intent the offence of unlawfully and maliciously causing GRIEVOUS BODILY HARM.

writ a court order commanding some action or forbearance.

Writer to the Signet a member of the oldest society of solicitors in Scotland, also known as *Clerk to the Signet.*

writ of execution a WRIT by which court judgments and orders are enforced.

writ of summons a WRIT that commences an action in the High Court.

wrongful dismissal the dismissal of an employee without justification and in breach of contract. *See also* UNFAIR DISMISSAL.

Y

young adult offenders offenders between the ages of 17 and 20, to whom special types of custodial treatment may apply.

young offenders *see* JUVENILE OFFENDERS.

youth court *see* JUVENILE COURT.

Z

zealous witness a WITNESS who attempts to give EVIDENCE as favourable as possible to one party in proceedings.